Angels
WHISPER

'Whose life is it, anyway?'

KATE O'KANE

Order this book online at www.trafford.com
or email orders@trafford.com

Most Trafford titles are also available at major online book retailers.

Printed in the United States of America.

ISBN: 978-1-4669-6718-2 (sc)
ISBN: 978-1-4669-6719-9 (e)

Trafford rev. 11/07/2012

 www.trafford.com

North America & international
toll-free: 1 888 232 4444 (USA & Canada)
phone: 250 383 6864 ♦ fax: 812 355 4082

To my husband Eddie who continues to walk the path of life with me, through thick and thin, through ups and downs!

Contents

Words of profound affirmation

God: *'Love one another as I have loved you. Love your neighbour as yourself.'*

Leonard Cohen: *'Only when something is broken, can the light get in! I have tried to be miserable, but cheerfulness kept breaking through.'*

Helen Keller: *'I thank God for my handicaps, for through them, I have found myself, my work, my God.'*

Eleanor Roosevelt: *'People grow through experience if they meet life honestly and courageously. This is how character is built.'*

Dorothy Day: *'If I have achieved anything in my life, it is because I have not been embarrassed to talk about God.'*

Ralph Waldo Emerson: *'To be yourself in a world that is constantly trying to make you something else is the greatest accomplishment.'*

St. Teresa of Avila: *'Let nothing trouble you, let nothing frighten you. All things are passing; God never changes.'*

My parents: *'Saints are made out of sinners who kept on trying.'*

Wake up Call!

Wake up!
Such words frequently tease everyone from time to time but do we hear and respond? The 'wake up call' may be in the form of gut reaction to an encounter or an experience, or just a feeling that seeks attention, or an image or picture we have seen and/or possibly something someone has said during a social or spiritual gathering.

All too often we are so consumed with the demands of life and living that such nudges are unintentionally ignored.

In the silence if you listen, you may just hear Angels whisper: 'Whose life is it anyway?'

Life is so often driven by many agendas: mine, his/hers, theirs and so on. Do this, do that, go here, go there which often we do without a single thought, till it comes to a time when we suffer fatigue which triggers off angst, illness and more. In life everyone has choice.

Are we blind and deaf to the invitation to 'wake up'? Do we react? How do we react?

So much of how we respond and act is as a result of the way we were reared and taught. For generations, fear and guilt have played a big part in life as a rule. God was portrayed as an ogre rather than a friend, one who could look beyond our faults, shortcomings and down falls and embrace us in unconditional love.

As life evolves we learn to unlearn and in so doing we have the opportunity to grasp the reins of responsibility for life and living.

When we open our hearts and our minds, the realness of spirit can penetrate our being. Furthermore, we no longer feel dictated to and driven by the influence of everyone else. We are invited to think and act for ourselves, bolstered rather than led, with the support of external beliefs and tradition.

There is so much help available to enhance and empower our wholeness of self.

Just pause for a moment and consider:

Who or what pulls at your heart strings?
Who or what pushes your buttons?
Who tramps on your toes?
Who or what makes you feel low?
Who or what helps you feel good?
Do you just say 'yes' when you really mean 'no'?
Do you just say 'no' when you really mean 'yes'?
Do you dare to believe in Angels?
Do you worry what others may say or think?
Why do you fear what others may say?
Why should you deny yourself God's love?
Why feel less than those that you encounter?

Did you do this, that or the other?
Did you go here, there, wherever?

Hey!
Look at yourself, you are who you are!
You are what you are!

 *Introduction*

The idea that life and the existence of the Angels go together may be difficult for some people to comprehend. However, somewhere it is possible to realise that there is some truth in this statement. When all seems dark and gloomy and life struggles to embrace the existence of light, the powerful energy of the Angels can emit that which is uplifting and empowering.

Frequently, life and living presents many happenings which necessitate due consideration.

Yet, sometimes it is difficult to know what to do. All too often, our basic humanness gives way to external influences when fear of what others may think affects personal choice and decision making.

At such a point that one fundamental question is posed: *'Whose life is it, anyway?'*

The aim of this book is not to dictate or coerce anyone in a predetermined manner, or to think in a particular way. It is an invitation to individuals searching for affirmation to consider and avail of contemporary therapies and spiritual support, to enhance and develop ultimate wellbeing: body, soul and mind.

Life throws so much at each and everyone of us, irrespective of colour, class, culture or creed. Even those, whom we aspire to, whether famous, influential and/or highly respectable, believe it or not, they too struggle with the dilemmas of life and living! Examples of such present themselves daily through the media, newspapers, magazines and personal encounters.

Don't be fooled, even the best can stumble.

All too frequently, life is like a mine-field.

Sometimes, everything seems so easy and all of a sudden without any warning, the carpet can so easily be pulled from beneath your feet, so to speak! Even those who imagine themselves to be well prepared, in control, and/or those publicly admired, may fall foul to the unknown path of life and living, encompassing the light and the dark, the thick and the thin threads and textures reflective of life's experiences.

Indeed, the Scriptures illustrate the human struggle and temptations Jesus himself had experienced while he journeyed upon earth.

Jesus experienced the mix of life and living, the ups and the downs. He spent time with his friends, instructing and encouraging people to be liberated. Frequently, Jesus felt the pain of abandonment, hurt, and rejection. For example, when He cried out *'My God, my God, why have you forsaken me'* and again *'Father take this Chalice from me?'* and yet in humble obedience, Jesus surrendered to the will of His Father, when he said *'Into your hands Lord, I commend my Spirit',* and *'Thy, will be done'.*

How wonderful it is to realise that our journey is frequently reflective of the ups and downs which Jesus himself experienced? The challenge is to surrender, hand all over to the Divine and trust. Yes! This is indeed a big ask, but there is nothing asked of anyone that cannot be realized.

In contemporary society, most people are searching; some don't have any idea of what it is that they need or really want. This was exemplified at a body, soul and mind conference a short time ago when a group of women in their mid fifties gathered to hear and receive information and support in relation to the body, soul and mind.

It was mind boggling!

Some women were very vocal and excited.

Many openly shared their concerns, their fear and unease. Some were quiet and exhibited a sense of apprehension. Some were hesitant to move beyond tradition and teachings. Fears of what others may think seemed to play a major role. And again, the fundamental question was asked:

'Whose life is it, anyway?'

Learning to unlearn was identified as an important consideration. Therapies of various sorts including alternative, complementary and traditional treatments were discussed. Scripture and the concept of Angels were tentatively broached, eventually giving way to a potentially positive transformation of mindset.

Can you identify with this?

Church teachings were considered and such gave way to an opening of mind and heart as sacred reflections provide great solace and hope. *'There are many rooms in my Father's house; I shall go before you to prepare a place for you'.* Such affirmation!

No strings!

No conditions!

Imagine, a place is being prepared for you, for me! We are invited to surrender and not to yield to distrust and/or doubt but rather to acknowledge our humanness and embrace all the help and support there is available.

Frequently, it was the presence of the Angels which brought great peace and comfort, bringing messages founded in Good News. The Angelic whispers can be received when we allow ourselves to be open to believe!

Angelic Whispers

Sometimes, we secretly ask the question, '*Who or what helped us through a particular event or happening?*' Occasionally, we are unaware of the spirit that illuminates the path: when it seems that we can't cope or understand what is being asked of us, yet, for some unknown reason we survive! When Angels are permitted to guide and protect, the fundamental everyday chores no longer seem so demanding. Things perceived to be great problems begin to subside in nature and design. Angels bring only that which is of a good vein into one's life, feeding the body, soul and mind with that which is of God.

Angels will never unnerve you.

True messages of love and hope will transpose negative attitudes and thinking. Afterall, God Himself frequented the most unlikely places and sat and drank with people looked down upon by society. Jesus permitted Mary Magdalene who was publicly referred to as a prostitute to sit by Him and wash His feet with the finest oil and dry His feet with her hair!

What about that then?

And when Zachariah, the tax collector disliked by the community, hid from the crowds, but Jesus saw him and invited him to dine with Him. Jesus used parables, stories, so that we might consider that when a seed is planted such may be overcome by the density of weeds; but with tenderness and due care, such can be harvested and saved. So too, as Christians we are planted as it were into the universe and in developing, many unwarranted encounters, events and discoveries yield the true harvest of one's being. Sometimes, we fail to realise that God's love for us is unconditional. And as in the examples of such, we can identify with the Angelic whispers that alert us to *'be'*.

Isn't the Bible containing the *'Word'* a great point of reference for one searching for confirmation in relation to God and the Angels?

There is little argument that within contemporary society there is a careful and somewhat tentative interest in the notion that Angels do exist. *'You got to be joking'* a close friend said when I first talked about the power of the Angels and how they impact upon each and everyone of us.

When hiccups occurred as they do, she would say *'Where are your Angels now then?'*, until one day this same person found a feather as she opened the front door where she found a letter she was waiting on from the hospital: *'As I tore open the envelope and nervously scanned the printed words: Your routine mammogram is all clear, then I remembered the little feather which I had picked up on my way into the house'*. So, in time she has allowed herself to believe in the heavenly messengers of God and the power they bestow.

The New Age approach to wellbeing is worthy of acknowledgement, yet, there is a tentative acceptance of such. Therapies of various forms have become apparent and such has overwhelmed many of us as we try to decide the legitimacy of what is on offer.

The realities and demands of life affect everyone and we all need someone or something to hold on to, to trust! In what is perceived to be a very progressive world there is an underlying aggressive creature lurking. So much poverty exists, which is widely documented. Yet, do we consider emotional poverty, lack of self belief and/or spiritual poverty?

Are we aware of the mask frequently worn which conceals the pain and hurt of the past, which is stored deep within?

We all strive for happiness and we can attain what is for our highest good when we open ourselves to the Spirit of God and allow the Angels to help and support us.

The ultimate goal of achieving personal inner peace and ultimate wholeness of self, well-being is a personal mission. Therefore, we are challenged to ask are we living in a world of idealism or realism; is this notion of achieving wholeness of self an accessible goal or is such perceived as a futile phenomenon?

Taking into consideration the diverse and complex society in which we live, we experience the struggle to win the fight and avoid the temptation to run away.

There is so much more help nowadays than one can ever imagine. For those who embrace the concept of *'healing'* it is fair to suggest that they are willing and open to believing in the concept of self help, which will eventually have a beneficial effect that will reach out to those around them.

As a relatively new phenomenon such a concept may require one to change their attitudes and mindset in regards to self-help.

Unlearning old beliefs, gives way to a new understanding and acceptance that such will emerge, that such can happen. Alternative and complementary therapies and methods are employed to enhance life and living, and a greater openness and acceptance to self help tools and remedies are worthy of consideration.

Grounded in Christianity and Faith, therapies have powerful effects in relation to wholeness of self. The secret is that anything that is of a positive energy will only yield that which is for one's highest good.

That which is suspect will allow the inner alarm bells to ring. Gut reaction frequently triggers a need to make an appropriate decision whether to participate or not in something new.

Initially, reflexology, acupuncture, body massage, Indian head massage, Reiki, energy healing of the chakras and/or the cellular memory, all have had to move at a rather unhurried pace before being accepted and acknowledged as an authentic means of healing.

To acknowledge that God is within everything is the basis of liberty. Everyone has the choice to believe, however, the context of my research, is based on a Christian belief, in which the Angels play an important spiritual role.

The inclusion of God's influence within the sphere of healing can only bring about that which is for one's highest good. Therefore, anything that can help to make better can only be of God.

If we believe that we are worthy, we can become aware of the power of the Angels whom God has created and given to each and everyone who dares to pause, to pray and to receive. Frequently, we are nudged to try something new, or receive a sign or a symbol which creates a sense of affirmation; even something as simple as a sweet smell when there are no flowers to be seen, can be a sign of a spiritual presence; or when someone hears their name being called when there is no-one around and/or a feather falls upon one's path. Even a song or tune that persists as you go about your work, can be enough to affirm one's belief that there is an Angel nearby!

The idea of *'parking Angels'* is widely practised by so many people. In recent times I have got to a point that before I even leave the house I specifically ask the Angels to go ahead of me to secure a parking space.

Some people laugh, but it works.

My most recent personal experience of such was one morning when I realised I was running late for a doctor's appointment.

I looked at the time: which read 10.25a.m.

I was so fixated with the need to get to my appointment that I whispered, *'Angels, I know I torture you, but, I need a parking space near the Parish Hall'*. As I patiently waited for the traffic lights to change to green I could see it was approaching 10.28. Passing the Health Centre I turned left towards the Parish Hall and there it was—a free parking space just for me. As I parked the car, I whispered *'thank you Angels'* that which I never fail to say.

I guess it is fair to say, that we all at some time or another, have had experiences which we found strange or hard to explain. Often after an incident people might say *'I know my mum/dad is looking after me';* or *'somebody up there is looking out for me'* and so on.

An old cliché suggests that:
'Life is what you make it, so give life a chance'.
Likewise, *Angels are what God gives us,*
So give Angels a chance'!

As in silence they, the Angels whisper—
'Whose life is it, anyway?'

# Whose life is it anyway?

Whose life is it anyway?

This question is one that everyone considers at some point in life. There is so much to contend with, from the innocence of childhood through adolescence into adulthood and the challenges associated with old age.

From time to time the encounters and the experiences are encouraging and full of hope. Every so often events and occurrences are threatening and challenging.

The circle of life and living frequently reflects a roller coaster or maybe a merry-go-round. The former is indicative of the ups and downs of life and the latter is reflective of how people enter and exit in and out of one's life.

Through generations there has been an emphasis on rules and directives which continue to shift in ordinance over time.

Sometimes, such may seem extreme, sacrosanct and demanding. Styles, fashion and trends continue to challenge everyone. Similarly, faith, tradition and culture are ever evolving.

All too often, it may seem that life deals out such a diverse spread of good and not so good happenings. But is it fair to suggest that in one's vulnerability, it is more human to focus on the negative more so than the positive occurrences which arise?

Life is full of contradictions.

Whether overt or covert, life's paradox is real: there is no hiding place, the inconsistencies frequently seek attention.

On the one hand, there is the belief or at least the invitation to suppose that everyone has the gift of '*free will.*' Yet, on the other hand, life is expected to be lived out, through a labyrinth of '*do's' and 'don'ts*'.

Dichotomies exist in practically everything including expectations, behaviour, education, religion: all of which demand decision making on a personal level. We have a responsibility to search for the best while living with the belief that each of us has the right to employ '*free will*', a gift highly respected by God and our spiritual guardians.

When new life is created, frequently, we overlook the fact, that before conception this soul has been designed by God with a mission to be fulfilled. Parents are caretakers of God's creation: such a wonderful accolade, to be chosen to be the earth guardians of God's creation.

To assist in the journey of life and living, every human being comes into this planet called earth, with the assistance of at least one Guardian Angel. The spirit friend assigned to each mortal being has the charge of guiding and protecting the body, soul and mind of the one under their care, especially when in a time of need.

It is a person's choice whether to avail of the assistance available brought about by the power of God's personal messenger.

Everyone has the gift of an Angel!

Yes, that's a fact.

Angels may very well reveal themselves in various ways, in ways you may never imagine. With an open mind and an open heart, it is unbelievable how an individual may be transmuted into a powerful positive being.

The presence of a spiritual aide may come in the form of a person whom we encounter; as a result of hearing the deep story of another; in the words of a song which repeat over and over in your mind; through a piece of music which helps to sustain you and empower your peacefulness; the image of an Angel or a Saint or even quiet communication within the silence of a serene setting: in Church, in a prayer space, at the beach or while hill walking or meandering through the woods. Nature frequently brings a profound closeness to the spirit of creation, God.

Showy winged Angels, accompanied with auras of brilliant light that figuratively symbolize the free will and lightness of the spirit, emphasise the inner weightlessness which we generally and unintentionally overlook when we entertain worry, anxiety, pain, fear, anger, frustration, stress, all of which may eventually manifest in some form of sickness or disease!

Everyone is afforded the respect to affect their '*free will*'; it is an individual choice to ask for help or to push aside that which is readily available. When confronted with tragedy, illness and/or discord there is always assistance in the form of unconditional love, God!

With the fragility of humanity, challenged by worldly rules and regulations set upon us, very often the existence of an imbalance between the spirit world and the earth collide.

The bridge between heaven and earth resembles the liberal movement of a swinging bridge, a span suspended over the waters which flow below and responding to the natural spheres of weather, which tend to change spontaneously. Thus, affecting its movement, similar to the regulations set upon us which affect how we perform and react.

It becomes more and more obvious from time to time, that, the contradictions associated with life and living is only an obstacle if we allow such to be. Overall wellbeing is dependent on the attitude, belief and understanding that there is nothing which doesn't pass.

All things pass!

Despite the directives which challenge us, we must keep in mind the fact, that we have choice. We are permitted to consider what is best. That which appears so simple on the surface may actually prove to be quite the opposite. In essence, what may appear to be a positive may very well be a negative and vice versa.

A difficult concept to comprehend!

After all, in society, whether it is State, Community, Health, Religion and/or Politics, there are guidelines and restrictions. Such are not set up for fun but rather as a means of protection, support and security for everyone.

However, in reality, it may be difficult to continue to believe that the adherence to the rules and regulations are of paramount importance where *'free will'* may not be an option!

Yet, *'free will'* is yours, ours!

Simple, yet challenging!

That which is perceived to be contradictory may very well be of our own making? Ultimately, just as life and living is the remit of every individual, so too, is the acceptance and use of the gift of *'free will'*. Therefore, when we deliberate on the *'do's' and 'don'ts'* set upon us by State, Society and Church and more, it may seem we are constantly challenged to be true to our *'free will, free choice!'*

Consequence brings choices and choices bring consequence. So, the challenge is to use the gift of *'free will'* and live within the parameters set out to serve as a protection and support.

Likewise, we are invited to make the appropriate choices in relation to ultimate wellbeing, as we are encouraged to serve the body, soul and mind the best there is on offer.

We are challenged to consider: *'Whose life is it, anyway?'*

After which one can claim that *'Life is yours, life is mine'* and acknowledge that *'Angels are yours, Angels are mine*

Life is yours, life is mine!
Angels are yours, Angels
are mine!

Life is an open canvas to be completed over a period of time. Life is painted by various shades and colours reflecting the joys and the sorrows of life and living, which we all encounter from time to time. Light and darkness, transparency and obscurity, sparkle and murkiness are all intermittent spheres which challenge everyone at some point in life.

Life is akin to a scratch card, when we scratch the surface reality is revealed.

Life is!

Life is for living!

Life is to be embraced and to be embodied with the support of God, the Angels, the higher power in accord with the rules and regulations of all that purports to make up the whole of society.

Can you begin to identify with such or are these assumptions too incredible to entertain or consider as authentic and/or legitimate. As life is generally dynamic, vibrant and challenging in nature, the human existence is based on the fundamental choice of *'fight or flight'*.

We are as good or as bad as we permit ourselves to be.

We can choose to claim the best, whether directly or indirectly, and/or we can permit others to influence and/or label us. For those who choose to believe, life is continuously accompanied by God's gift of an Angel. This is not for a select few but for every human being who dares to believe.

Go on, claim that which is yours: the light, the spirit and the love of God, brought about by messengers clothed in the Spirit.

As baptized Christians, we are afforded the gift of *'free choice'* and given responsibility for life and living. At a group meeting recently, one member suggested that *'Some people would argue that to be baptized was not their choice'*; perhaps it is a fair statement or on the other hand maybe it is a cop-out or a crutch to have something to lean on when choosing not to conform to directives as laid down by tradition. Such can affect change.

Either way, what is clear from a Christian perspective is that, God created each and everyone of us and unlike any other species such as animals, birds, fish and plants; we human beings have the choice to discern and choose the best help available to grow in the body, soul and mind.

We are encouraged to acknowledge and become aware, accept and appreciate that life is to be lived, to be nourished and to be enjoyed. Being armoured with the Spirit of God, we have the choice to ask for help, not just for the soul, but for the betterment of one's entire wellbeing.

In Scriptures we are told there are tools which are there to help build and repair that in need. Similarly in contemporary society there is a wealth of tools readily available to help attain ultimate wellbeing: therapies wearing a wide range of labels, offering help and support to one in need!

Angels provide us with energy too incredible to describe. And the process is so simple: just call!

The invitation is for everyone.

There are no conditions, and there is never any judgement or measuring stick.

God accepts us as we are, not where we think He would like us to be!

Do you believe that?

Can you honestly allow yourself to be free? Can you completely trust that God loves you as you are? And that the Angels will carry you through the challenging times as such occurs?

When times are good we rarely pause to think that an unheard, unseen spirit helped to illuminate the path. Unseen, unheard, these powerful aides come in many various forms: people we encounter from time to time, those who greet one another with a smile or a kind word; those who help to carry a bag, hold a door open, and give someone a seat and/or step aside to let someone pass by.

Such gestures may mean so much, similar to the acorn which eventually grows into a great oak tree that expands its branches reaching out to all around.

Angels too, reach out to all around.

When we can accept that Angels are God's gift to each and everyone, we can believe that such ultimately sustains, empowers and leads to true inner peace.

To call upon an Angel for assistance is not for any one person, more than another. To seek help, whether therapy for the body, soul and/or mind, must never to be perceived to be a sign of weakness, but rather a sign of strength, reflective of maturity and responsibility of self development and attainment of ultimate wellbeing!

Therefore, don't delay, sure if you don't ask you can't receive! How can we expect to get what we want or need if we don't ask?

God is not a mind reader!

Angels wait upon your supplication!

Even your closest friend can't read your mind!

Jesus said: *'Ask and you shall receive.'*

So when we ask rest and wait in a blessed state of anticipation, God's messengers, the Angels will respond bringing about that which is for one's highest good. How could we receive that which we desire if we don't first of all identify what it is that we seek and then make a specific request to the relevant body (be it a need for spiritual/religious support; or help to heal a physical, mental or emotional condition)?

If we suffer ill health we can't expect a doctor to know, if he/she is not adequately informed of what one is experiencing. When someone finds themselves out of work or lacking in finance, how can such be deal with if one doesn't ask for help!

Just stop!

If any of us want help from someone, surely we could not expect that they should know what it is that we need. No matter how well we know someone, we could not expect them to know exactly what we need or want. Therefore, is it fair to suggest that it is appropriate to ask!

Likewise, God wishes purely to help but in reality we have the choice whether to ask for help or not. Just akin to human friends, God, the Angels and the Ascended Masters (Saints and holy people who have walked upon this world), need to be made aware of one's request!

So just call!

Spiritual aides communicate on our behalf to God, who is resident permanently within one's soul. Pure intention yields a rich harvest.

When we ask with pure heart there is no doubt, what is for one's highest good does emerge!

Yeah!

Believe it or not, all we have to do is to call upon the Angels who consistently listen, hear and promptly react, so as to assist us.

It is a myth to consider that certain people are chosen to see, to meet and to work with the Angels. There is no human being any more deserving of the Angelic presence than another.

To experience the existence of the Angels there are no bench marks.

There is no X factor involved.

Angels are with us while we work, rest and play. Angels surround us in *the ups and the downs* of life and living. As Angels wait, they are with us constantly: Angels are with us when we awaken and rise to greet the day. Angels are with us when we prepare to go to sleep.

They, the Angels are excited when we pray to greet them as the morning sun rises and when we pray in thanksgiving as the moon fills the night sky. When sickness is experienced, there is much to be experienced when we surrender.

While visiting a patient in the Hospice, the terminally ill person, despite pain and suffering said *'When I gaze out at the night sky and watch the stars twinkle, it is then that I know that the Angels are blowing kisses to all who are open to receive God's love'*.

How wonderful!

In the midst of what many would find hard to endure, this person could see beyond that which was drawing life from within. Cancer did not block the depth of spirit of this being.

Therefore, as in the words of a hymn composed by Steve Warner *'Set your sights on the highest gifts; faith, hope and love and the greatest is love!'*, the invitation is to believe, to recognise and to reach out and claim the best on offer. God's gifts of life and a spiritual guide, an Angel, are more precious than words may possibly describe. Take up the challenge, there is nothing impossible with the belief and acceptance that there is a provision in which the wholeness of self may be enhanced, enriched and embraced.

Don't be afraid!

God who created you, me, us, will never abandon His own! Jesus said *'Do not be afraid, I am with you always, yes, even to the end of time'*.

Hence, affirmation that we are never alone!

It is our choice to connect with the spirits who wait to serve. God, the Angels and the Ascended Masters are not magical; as such spirits are mindful of our *'free will'* to choose and with respect for such, cannot and must not, intervene without an invitation!

We have the choice to believe!

In believing we receive and in receiving we are blessed and embraced in *'faith, hope and love'*, gifts we are invited to set our sights upon: the highest gifts. Open your heart and receive!

The invitation is to embrace the fact that *'life is yours, life is mine'* and to believe that life is to be lived to the full.

Life is . . . . !

Life . . . what is life?

Life is yours, life is mine!

Life is a gift in which we exist upon this planet we call earth. Life is an invitation to live, to contribute to the development of self. When taken seriously, we have a responsibility to seek the best of everything available, that is, everything that can make life easier, enhance self and assist to make life more manageable.

Life is a gift from God . . . we are born of the Spirit . . . yeah we can guide, we can direct, we can support but all must come from the profound source of love for one and another, not the way we perceive it should or ought to be, not where we think a person should be or ought to be, but where a person is at. Then and only then can any help and/or guidance be offered.

Nothing comes from nothing!

Therefore everything is founded from something!

Everything is designed to challenge us to be real, to realise that when things work contrary to the way we expect or want, with patience and belief, it will become obvious to all that all things work out: what is for one's highest good will materialize. We learn to realise and understand that there are reasons for everything. When we are calm, the bigger picture can emerge. But when we invoke or entertain anger and/or frustration, the whole scenario becomes blurred and even somewhat alarming. It is easy to slip into that negative space where apathy drives the mind, permitting complex expectations to emerge.

Isn't it strange how expectations can affect us! Expectations can be quite basic and attainable, yet, on the other hand, quite the opposite may be apparent where the contrast may be quite surreal. Therefore, we are confronted with a need to interpret the demands and the expectations of life, and if such are really worthy of attention.

When something is addressed and attended to, quite often what seemed insurmountable can begin to be realised as not such a big deal, after all. When all is going well, it is quite easy to drift along aimlessly; life may appear to be uncomplicated and clear cut.

It is difficult to consider what *'might be'* irrespective of how anyone is feeling. At such times, it seems that we can do everything ourselves. We are so confident that we can't possibly consider that there is any need for God, never mind family or friends. It is appreciated that we believe in God but maybe we don't feel He can make things any better for us: in such instance God is sited in a safe place, as a treasure stored away.

Yet, is it fair to suggest that frequently, that which is placed *'out of sight'* has the potential to remain *'out of mind'* with the potential to be forgotten for some reason until someone or something triggers off a reminder of its existence. *'Out of sight, out of mind'* is a general rule of thumb. So, just as God may be packed away in safe keeping, occasionally we are invited to seek His help. It is possible to realise the power of the Angels and recognize what Angels can do for us.

It is good to know and believe that help is always at hand even if God is temporarily tucked safely away?

How often have you felt that the world was falling in around you? Have you felt that the dark overwhelms the mind and there is the possibility that, that which is *'out of sight and out of mind'* is lost? The inactivity of such treasures can be detrimental especially when the blanket of the night dares to entrap the fragility of the mind.

Is it fair to suggest that when everything appears to be overshadowed with the blackening cloud encasing us, we can't even think straight never mind make choices?

The darkness houses the deep pain and hurt of that which we experience from time to time.

On a visit to a housing campus, a middle-aged man asked *'How do you know when God is at home?'* Thinking this was a joke I waited for the punch line; to eventually realise such was not a joke but a legitimate question. He freely shared his story of how he allowed his life to be abused with the negative use of alcohol.

Life didn't seem to mean much, he was so angry and he just couldn't say sorry for the discord he had created.

Everybody else was to blame.

And, God got a touch too!

At this juncture the man continued *'I have been praying and am tired waiting on an answer. It seems to me*

God is just like everyone else, either he's not at home or I am put on hold.

I stopped going to chapel a couple of years ago 'cause I lost everything and I blame him for everything'. This angry man's rant went on . . . . in time the topic regarding Angels raised its head . . .

'And as for Angels, well I'm not sure. But, I think there is something in it. The other day I put in a wash, turned on the washing machine . . . nothing happened! . . . . A first for me in a long, long time, I actually prayed. I asked these so called Angels every body's talking about, to help.

I walked up the corridor towards my room. And as I did a white feather appeared out of nowhere. It was so perfect, small and frail! Well can you imagine what that meant to me? I believed this was a sign that the Angels were on my case. As I turned back I could hear the washing machine beginning to splutter and spit, as it began the wash cycle. For once something good happened'.

Had this little feather ignited a renewed sense of belief for this person who struggled with his faith? Sometimes, we dismiss the little things that happen, the little signs we receive. In reality it is each small thing or happening which eventually builds into something great, something of worth. Frequently it is only when we encounter positive happenings that we can begin to understand the power and the actions of the Angels. Some people are unresponsive to the notion that there is help available. Yet, for those who permit themselves to open their hearts and their minds to transformation, happenings of any nature no longer throw us into a state of helplessness and fear. This doesn't mean that we are alien from the realness of life and living but rather that we are better equipped to deal with that which we come to face-to-face.

Sure if we are not sick, depressed or broken, in reality we don't pause to think what life may be like, if everything was to be reversed.

Can you identify with this?

Similarly, if we don't invite the Angels to embody us, we can never know the immeasurable love and service we deny ourselves.

Can you understand the power of the Angels and allow them into your lives to bridge the gap between dark and light, depth and height and/or the right and the wrong deluding us?

It is an invitation to all, to be open to constructive criticism and affirmative guidance, which help us discern the right way forward. We all need some kind of guidance and undoubtedly develop positively with affirmative comments and appropriate recognition.

Sure don't we all like to hear compliments?

We grow and glow when we hear positive comments, we may act shy but somewhere deep within words of affirmation have a positive effect upon self development. When people acknowledge us and appreciate our contribution, whatever the circumstance, now don't tell me we shrug such off. Positive comments are uplifting and empowering influences, which everyone benefits from, whether directly or indirectly.

Yet, for some unknown reason we frequently experience quite the opposite which causes disquiet within the very core of our being. People nursing anger, hurt, jealousy or some other form of negativity frequently lash out at those whom they think to be better than them.

Stop!

No-one is better than anyone else.

This is a fact. It is we ourselves who permit others to affect us. Circumstances play a vital role in how we perceive ourselves and others to 'be'. When negative thoughts are given life, the spiral affect has the potential to create a famine which has occurred within the contemporary church. There will always be those using negativity to erode peace. The harmony of body, soul and mind are dependent on many factors which we have the power to address or ignore.

Have you experienced an occurrence in which your faith has been shaken or almost shattered? Have you allowed society to steer you along life's path? Have you paused to take stock and see what is really happening? Have you taken control of your own destiny? Have you opened the curtains covering the eyes of your body, soul and mind? Have you allowed the shadows of the past to block out the light? When the darkness overshadows the light, it seems that you are swimming against the tide and you fear being pulled or dragged down into an abyss. When you reflect, it is normal enough to torture yourself to find a reason why you feel the way you do and ask yourself over and over again, how did you deal with this or that or the other and so on!

Can you become aware of the possibility that the words, the actions and/or the approval of others occasionally impact negatively upon us; that occasionally the temptation is to withdraw rather than stand firm; run away rather than stand tall and to show the world the strength of your being.

The images of climbing the cliff face reflect how many of us almost reach the top and repeatedly slip back. The challenge is to try to climb again and again, until we reach the top.

The Angels are always ready to help you to claim your right to resolve that which challenges you. The messengers of God, the Angels, invite you to ask for their help. When you are confronted with something that seems too awful to be resolved, you are encouraged to believe that help is at hand. There is never anything too big or too small that God and the Angels can't restore.

The fundamental requisite is to have the faith to believe. Belief gives way to hope, and hope generates love. In reality we are all at liberty to embrace faith, hope and love. Life doesn't have to be an isolated or lonely journey; the choice is yours, ours and mine. When we embrace the support of other people, family, friends and carers, life will yield fruit in plenty. There will be an abundance of support and help.

However, if we choose to push people aside, hold grudges, and nurse old wounds, it is almost impossible to notice or to get pleasure from support which is available. If we choose not to bother about other people, inevitably through time people will react in kind. When anyone ignores the help on offer, irrespective of what kind of support or from whom, how can anyone expect people to worry about them?

If we are reluctant to allow change to occur, then we deny ourselves the chance to heal that which is broken or bruised within self; sometimes it may be difficult to believe that inner damage caused by hurt, pain, and/or abuse, has the potential to permit disease to manifest itself in some form whether it be physical, psychological or spiritual.

All life is valuable and consequently, such deserves due respect irrespective of status . . . in lay terms there are no persons better nor worse than you, we, me. What is important is to note and to beware of what lies within each of us. We must take the responsibility for that which we give to those wearing labels; human beings whom we empower to either respect or abuse us.

Nature fights for survival and without criticism there is always the potential to allow people to confuse assertiveness with aggressiveness. Status refers to one's standing, position, rank, grade within society, within community and/or establishments designed to help to make life and living better for everyone. Sometimes, the line between one's place of prominence and one's reputation may be either misinterpreted or misused within various situations and shakes the confidence of the searching soul.

Ultimately, it is so easy to permit others to sap our energy, to have the power to append their agenda onto us. Just detach and in the silence hear the Angels whisper:

'Hey! Whose life is it anyway?
Wake up, smell the coffee!'

Reclaim the power, reawaken the sense of self and embrace the reality that in essence *'Life is yours, Life is mine!'*

Ultimately, there is no directive but an invitation to believe that *'Angels are yours, Angels are mine'.*

# Angels are . . . !

Angels are yours.
Angels are mine!
Angels—can they help?
Can Angels support us?
What can Angels do for you, for me, for us?

Angels can't direct or influence your thoughts, words or deeds, so what can Angels do for you, for me, for us? As they wait, they sing which is how they praise God. In their prayers they intercede for you, for me, for us. Can you begin to imagine the excitement when the Angels hear you call upon them for help! However, when not availing of the spiritual support available, there is the possibility that external influences may negatively impact upon you.

So who has the greatest influence?

You yourself or do others have control to drive your life along the path whether rough or smooth! External influences towards self development frequently affect all of us.

Do we allow such external pressures to direct us or can you dare to claim the power to allow the Angels into one's personal space?

With profound belief the ongoing work of the Angels will never fail to amaze you. These Heavenly beings wish only to assist. Their greatest wish is that everyone can be grace filled. When open to the notion that *'Angels are yours, Angels are mine'*, the interconnectedness between each other will develop in an authentic loving and gracious manner. God wants only the best and when we invite the Angels to help us we begin to acknowledge the unconditional love of God.

In essence, we are cherished human beings with support available on tap 24-7 365. As messengers of God, Angels wait for your call, my call . . . they will never interfere, intrude or interpose . . . Angels wish only to bring about that which is for one's highest good . . . Angels desire only to please us mortals, created in the image of God . . . . whose love for us is so profound that nothing only the best will suffice . . . . God loves each and everyone of us irrespective of colour, class, culture or creed!

If we can grasp the humility to accept that God wants nothing more than to love us, then the grace you will receive will help you to face anything. The Angels will work tirelessly when called upon to bring about that which is for your highest good.

What are Angels?

Angels are assigned to each human being not at birth, nor at conception but even before the process begins. God knows when we will be conceived, when we will be born, when we will die. God even decides where we are best placed and affords a mission to be achieved while journeying the path of life and living.

The plan is designed with great love. So, do we dare to think that the one, who creates each and everyone of us, would allow evil to destroy us!

No!

Is the precise answer . . . yet, we have our part to play. Would you, would I, repay someone we love by hurting them?

With even the tiniest grain of faith, it is worth realising that God wants to allow us to choose help. Believing that we have been given the gift of '*free will/free choice*', we are challenged to realise that God respects and trusts us to seek and find what is best for all ultimate wellbeing.

Now, be really honest, can you, can we say that we can manage on our own; can we honestly claim that we don't need anyone or anything? Truth be told, everyone needs help at some point; everyone is worthy of help, unconditional, non-judgemental support.

But do we really, really believe that?

Do we feed the hunger or do we play the big guy within company of family, friends, colleagues and more and then cry in the privacy and silence in that place apart?

In contemporary society we continually empower society to be the driving force rather than taking the reins to applaud your inner drive to travel the path of life and living in a way that allows your personal development blossom into maturity. Therefore, there is most definitely a challenge within contemporary society to walk the walk, and talk the talk, so as to allow one's self to '*be*', just to be ourselves and not tempted to be afraid to '*be*'. Despite the demands of society you, me, we have a responsibility to live life?

Are you determined to overcome the false ideologies concealed within that which we suppose to be cool? Can we believe that we can make decisions? Or do we shy away when we wish to live life that suits you, we, me or live a life not influenced by those around us?

Because of the conceited hidden agendas of many, we may very well be blind and deaf to the reality of being human and the ongoing demands that face each of us day and daily. Sometimes we just want to be liked and will adapt to please, to fit in and belong.

Waiting at the airport is one of those places where we can freely observe the diversity of humankind. It is in such a setting that we notice the diversity of individuals, gender, age, culture, colour and the consequential behaviour as each person awaits their pending journey.

The hustle and bustle can be quite disconcerting and overwhelming for many. Whether covert or overt, behaviour has a way of revealing the reality that lies within, even that of the stranger.

Stretched out upon the static set of four chairs, a young unshaven character shook himself as he arose into a sitting position beside me.

After a grunt and a snuffle, he asked *'What time is it?'* With a glance at my watch I replied *'It's just reading 14.44'*. His response was unexpected as he told me *'There is a sequence of numbers there, did you notice that?'* He took an Angel book out of his bag and looked up 1444, reading the Angel message associated with 144 followed by that of the number 4, which referred to positivity of thought and the affirmation and invitation to call upon the Angels for support and help. I was amazed. Here was a young man whom I never would have guessed to be interested in Angels sharing Angel messages with me.

(An example of how wrong one can be).

After reading the Angel message aloud, the topic of conversation was based upon the concept of Angels. He freely explained how his interest in Angels evolved and how his long standing problem with headaches was healed. *'One day as I was sitting at a desk, I experienced that which I can only describe as a bolt of lightning hitting my head. I fell off my chair and lay on the floor of the campus library. Aware of the commotion going on but somehow incapable of communicating with those around me, I had no choice other than to wait. Amid the excitement of those who had gathered there was a serenity that is indescribable, even today.*

There was a growing light, so bright that my eyes hurt. As the light fully emerged, the hustle and bustle around me seemed to fade away. The place I found myself to be in was so calm, I just didn't want to be disturbed' he said. I couldn't help asking *'Then what happened?'*

Looking at me he replied *'Well, I knew there was a presence of someone or something leaning over me. I couldn't identify what it was. There was indescribable warmth . . . then the vibrant light got so strong and there was the feeling that I was being drawn by some force alien to me. It was as if I were going further into a tunnel. I wasn't scared; it was so peaceful.*

Since that day, I have never suffered headaches and have been blessed with a renewed sense of faith, hope and love'.

It was affirmative to meet and to hear the personal story of one healed by the power of the Angels. One of the important points to note is that real friends do not place demands on one another. Close friends do not dictate but rather encourage each other's personal growth. Real friends are reflective of the Angels; they respect your choice and wait for an invitation to help.

Angelic Healing!

Angels appear in many forms: spiritual guardians, light workers, earth Angels who work from somewhere within the Heavenly sphere, which is beyond comprehension, yet, they serve without hesitation and act lovingly for those who call upon them for support and/or help. Maybe the Angels nudge us from time to time, but one thing is for sure, that frequently symbols and signs exemplify the Angels in action too. God's love is ours in abundance, liberally and unconditionally.

Angels serve only to bring about that which is for one's highest good.

The following story is an example of how Angels deliver that which is beneficial to one's wellbeing. *'A few years ago, after a minor accident, I was overwhelmed by the reaction of people whom I was only getting to know. Cards and flowers accompanied with 'good wishes' continually arrived as I recovered from the mishap at the class. In such acts, I had no doubt that God was at work; Angels conveyed a good sense of affirmation. I felt important and recovered very quickly.*

Deep within my mind the actions of such spirit filled people have indelibly imprinted upon my heart'. Angels deliver that which is for one's highest good and gives way to a profound sense of peaceful freedom and transformation. Angelic healing is God's answer to our prayer.

When we are aware, accept and appreciate the Angels and the therapies available to each and everyone of us.

Alternative therapy, complementary therapy and/or traditional medicine or alone, Angel therapy including prayer, signs and symbols, statues, candles and cards, and/or reflexology, energy healing and more, may greatly enhance the experience of achieving a more balanced life.

In addition to the afore mentioned, religious traditions including Christianity, Buddhism and Judaism and more too, recognise that prayer is a powerful source of support; prayer in various forms such as meditation, contemplation, Lectio Divina and devotional prayer are tools which help to nourish the soul.

Within a Christian context, the Scared Scriptures, the Psalms and the practice of sacred adoration serve as spiritual guidance yielding to a sense of spiritual convergence. It is true that nowadays, used as a mix or alone, therapies offer help and support.

It's a fortunate time and place to be for many interested in availing of what's on offer to assist in attaining the best for life and living: that which suffices to sustain the body, soul and mind!

Spiritual healing contributes to the healing of the body and mind and vice versa. Healing of any nature is impossible if one doesn't believe that such can occur. Transformation is essential to the development of self and the belief that there is a range of help available to enhance ultimate wellbeing of body, soul and mind.

Healing occurs when one is prepared to receive. With patience and profound belief healing can happen, such requires patience and openness to acceptance of what is for one's highest good. This is the promise associated with the gift of the Angels: as messengers of God, Angels serve to bring about that which is for one's highest good to you, me, and everyone. We all have at least one Angel; all we have to do is to believe and to have the humility to acknowledge our personal needs and ask for help.

Any form of healing, miracle or cure takes time. Nothing happens until God decides what it is that is for the best. With patience that which is paramount to a successful and appropriate outcome will emerge. Undoubtedly, there are people who experience extraordinary happenings and for some people healing does take place, miracles do happen. However, in such cases, there are factors to be considered: the nature of the condition, the illness, and/or the request. Quite often we are faced with challenges.

When Mary Anne was going to visit her daughter in hospital, she shared this story of an experience which she refers to as: *'A very definite Angel moment'. As I watched the countdown of the lift on its way to the ground floor I was unaware that anyone else was waiting. When I entered the lift, there stood a tall rather robust individual with short auburn hair. Trying to sneak a look, I could see he was quite handsome, clean shaven and not as young as his appearance suggested. Quietly he turned and glanced down on me before speaking.*

'Your little girl is in Ward 14c' he said.

I just stared at him. After what seemed an age, he continued, 'The tumour has gone, Rachael will be fine and by the way, a great name, may I say'. The lift then stopped abruptly, 'Doors opening, Level 7', the automated voice called out and as the man left a radiant green light filled the lift. 'Doors closing', the robotic female voice concluded.

I stood in the mirrored cubed space trying to make sense of my encounter while the lift seemed to fly up to level 14. As the doors opened there was angst in my step. It was as if I just couldn't wait to see Rachael'.

Mary Anne told how she deliberated on what had happened as she walked up the long corridor to the room where her ill daughter lay or so she thought!

'On entering the room I nearly dropped. It was just so surreal. To my surprise my little girl was running around the bed.

'Oh! My God', I shouted out as I watched my wee Princess. It was only late the day before that I was told the prognosis was not good.

I was excited.

But I was afraid!

Angelic healing was my profound request.

When my little Princess saw me, she ran towards me calling out excitedly, 'Mommy, mommy, there was a big tall man in to see me today! He looked like God, mommy. When he touched my head I felt as if my head was on fire. He gave me a present'. The story seemed unreal until Mary Anne saw her child open her wee Angel box and take out a small pale green feather.

'The minute I saw that wee feather I knew then who the big man was', Mary Anne continued.

'Doctor Hayne came towards us with a folder in her hand. 'Mary Anne will you take a seat'. Opening the folder a sheet of paper fell onto the ground which the doctor and myself reached for together. 'Well look at that, how did that get there?', Doctor Hayne said as a tiny picture of

St Raphael wearing a suit of armour and a mop of yellow hair lay under the folder? Then in a professional tone she started, 'You will be glad to hear this . . . We can't explain it just now but your wee lass has won the lottery, her tumour has not only shrunk but it's gone.

What more can I say?

We just don't have the answer at the minute but I think you may have your own notion,' she said as she winked and continued on with what the next tests would involve.

How much more affirmation could anyone want? It is clear that when we allow ourselves to believe in the higher power and presence of God, that which is for the highest good of the individual can happen. Occasionally, the outcome to a request may not necessarily reflect what is perceived as an appropriate response to the want or desire of the one in need. No prayer goes unanswered; granted the answer may not reflect the profound request but there is always something good to be found.

What we do experience is so valuable, much more valuable than one can ever imagine.

Believe it or not, in some instances we may think we haven't gotten that which we asked for; but in essence it will become clear, in time.

Trust!

Wait; believe . . . all things come to those who wait.

Take time to discern what you experience and then empower yourself to make the proper choice.

Try not to empower others to lead you to a place you would rather not go, don't be afraid, and be assertive. Glean on that rooted in God.

Contemporary society has much good to offer which can enhance the wholeness of self, highlight that which helps to motivate and maintain a balanced way of life and living. Unfortunately, so much emphasis is put onto the negative happenings, the conflict and the threat to the moral fibre of many aspects of modern day culture. Many facets are being attacked: institutions, professions, religion, and politics. In reality, there is little doubt that we often feel so inadequate that we become apathetic and believe we have no part to play.

O.K. we may nurse a notion that we are not adequately equipped to deal with this or that! Many people can relate to such, but, there is an invitation to seek help. Never underestimate the power of prayer, the tradition surrounding the Angels and the stories of affirmation recorded in Scripture. Likewise, the prayerful support of community can undoubtedly bolster those in need. Little encounters and experiences bound in love are of God. Yet, it is important to note that when one is vulnerable, the evil spirit may try to seduce a good person.

God said over and over again, '*Do not be afraid, I am with you*'. This phrase offers do much affirmation as we encounter the daily demands upon life and living.

Rest, listen and then act!

Frequently, we let fear become an overriding factor as we struggle to make appropriate decisions. When we struggle we look for signs. We succumb to various forms of apparent affirmation irrespective of its source. Fortune tellers, clairvoyants, psychics, horoscope, supernatural/ paranormal modes of communication endeavour to feed the hunger of vulnerable individuals. The legitimacy of such are not always sacrosanct, therefore, it is important to be aware of the authenticity of what is on offer. As messengers of God Angels wish to serve in an unconditional way, they reinforce God's message of hope as we are reminded that God is always with us and He invites us to believe and not to be afraid.

However, some people have difficulty with directives such as '*chain letters*'.

Don't be afraid.

If something doesn't sit comfortably with tradition and teachings, choose to disregard. Prayer can never be dependent on a directive that to receive x, y or z, such must be passed onto a number of other people. God will never promise *you this or that* if you pass such letters on; nor will anything untoward occur if *you don't do this or that,* as some letters may imply.

God's love for us is unconditional.

Prayer should never pose a threat.

Prayer is a powerful tool, prayer can be silent or verbal, but either way when said in the belief that God hears our plea, peace and serenity light the path of life and living.

Identifying and accepting that complete healing can be realised is a first step but the invitation is to continue to seek all that is good for the body, soul and mind. Always remember, if one part of one's being is not working, inevitably this will have a negative impact on the whole self akin to the domino effect, i.e. when one block falls, the effect is ongoing. The spin-off can be detrimental to full growth but never despair as long as one turns to God, all is not lost.

God's love is unconditional.

Therefore, we are encouraged to be aware, accept and appreciate the gift of an Angel, a guardian who oversees all that we encounter. In contemporary society there is a greater awareness, acceptance and appreciation of the power of Angels and the gift of guidance given by God to each one of us. As God is immortal, we are frequently reminded that the Angels were created to serve God and act on our behalf; Angels do not have the shortcomings of humans; they aim to bring God's peace and calmness into our lives. We can't worship Angels, but they love to be appreciated. When God sent forth his firstborn into the world, he says, *"Let all God's angels worship him" (Hebrews 1:6)* Angels are in the service of the Lord as we in turn are in service to humankind, to help to make this a better world.

So, just say a wee word of thanks to God and the Angels. Surely you know the effect such a word of gratitude can mean? So too, the Angels love to be acknowledged.

Never fail to be grateful for all the gifts and encounters that equip us to live out the Christian message: *'Love One God above all Gods and love thy neighbour as thyself.'*

These two of the Ten Commandments exemplify Love, a threefold invitation to Love God, thyself and thy neighbour and when we can embrace this concept, then life and living takes on a whole new meaning. We no longer waste valuable time seeking that which is unattainable, as with the eyes and ears of the body, soul and mind, the meaning of life and living is illuminated. When we become aware, accept and acknowledge the power of the Angels, we find it so much easier to know that God is within everyone we meet. At such a point the deep threefold love we have radiates out liberally to all that we experience and those we encounter.

Angels are akin to a bridge spanning the path between Heaven and Earth. The stairways to heaven twist and turn and rise at various points, so don't give up if you stumble, trip or fall. Just get up again, brush yourself down and try again as the spiritual gatekeepers explicitly serve.

# Angels: the gatekeepers

Angels are the gatekeepers/caretakers of the soul . . . . how wonderful is that?

How wonderful it is to know that we have our very own caretaker, yet, unlike a mortal caretaker, the Angels can't act, guide or direct, as they ultimately respect the gift of '*free will, the freedom of choice*', God has given to each and everyone of us, mortal human beings. It is God who sows the seeds of our lives and of our destiny but we have our part to play, we have the responsibility to tend to the weeds teasing to strangle the good within.

If the weeds are not attended to, eventually the weeds can become so problematic that they may strangle and destroy the potential growth of that which was planted.

Within the Angelic realm of Heaven, a number of Angels wait with great joy and quiet excitement with a duty to help human beings in need. Embrace the spiritual blossoms of the Angelic realm. The power of the Angelic Realm is one that is unseen and unheard. Angels,

Guardian Angels, Archangels and Ascended Masters are all representative of the presence of God

But can you allow yourself, myself, to rely on that which is unseen, unheard? The demands of life and living are indeed problematic.

However, with faith and growing belief things can only get better with the knowledge that there is help available to all. The most used phrase by Jesus in the Scriptures is one of invitation, one of hopeful affirmation: *'Do not be afraid, I am with you'*. Such a phrase broken into two parts: *'Do not be afraid'* which reminds us that there is no need to doubt, to worry or to become anxious. *'I am with you'* reminds us that you, me, we are never alone. We are invited not directed or dictated to; we are constantly being invited to feed our spiritual hunger and thirst from the well of heaven. Those who serve us from this well are the Archangels; Ascended Masters (Saints) and the Angels who mediate between us and God. The Angels surround us no matter where we are, no matter what we are doing. They patiently guide and protect us and are happiest when called upon to help or assist us in our times of need.

There are no conditions attached.

As anxiety, stress, fear, sadness, loneliness, and many other factors take centre stage in one's life, there is an invaluable wealth of spiritual support waiting to be called upon. We all struggle from time to time, that's life, but, we have the responsibility to claim the best. Occasionally, we are prompted by the Angels to ask ourselves, *'Whose life is it, anyway?'*

Can you identify with this?

God readily responds and gives those who call for help, an awareness of the abundance of Angelic guides waiting to assist those in need.

Call upon the Angels and allow them to work for you. Angels are happiest when they are busy. There are still some people who find that concept hard to believe. However, when a person is at rock bottom, or lonely, depressed or weary with fear and angst about sickness, death and things we can't control, it is at such times we need something to hold on to! As in the song *'Breakeven'* by *'The Script'*, *'I pray to a God, I don't believe in'*, a contradiction in kind but also an acknowledgement that when we have nothing else to hold on to, God is called upon.

Likewise, God's messengers eagerly await our call. Angels don't have control over us, they cannot intervene, they cannot attend to us as the mortal gardener attends his/her plants; not like the greenhouse keeper who can clear out, clean out the unwanted weeds which have the potential to choke the best of the plants being nurtured and encouraged to grow, to develop and to bloom to their full potential.

However, what happens if stones are thrown at the greenhouse/glass house? There is the potential to break and to spoil something of worth . . . people in glasshouses don't throw stones!

Why?

Those who live in glasshouses don't throw stones because they respect and appreciate their space. So too, we are invited to recognise and appreciate our space and to make the use of what is within our own space, our inner being.

Do we recognise the seeds we sow?

Do we want to recognise that which may consume our energies or make demands upon us?

Do we dare to believe that we may actually empower that which is not worthy of attention, the invitation into the dark clothed in fear, anxiety, pain, rejection, isolation and more?

What can we hope to receive to if we nurture the seeds of negativity? Dare we believe we shall yield a rich harvest of positivity?

'As ye sow, so shall ye reap.' (Galatians 6:7)

Sometimes we are so busy trying to please others that we deny ourselves the best available to us. When we stop and take stock: we are asked to listen to the positive invitation to *'be'* by God. It is at such a stage we know we are protected. Therefore, can you allow your guardian Angel to support you?

Can you overcome the powerful hold others may have upon you?

It is your/my prerogative to call upon the Angels for help and support, it is a personal choice whether to believe that Angels exist, that Angels listen and respond when called upon. We all have at least one Angel whom we refer to as our Guardian Angel; we are invited to trust this unseen and unheard spirit which is forever present.

It is heartening to realise that God is the Spiritual Gardener, it is He who sows the seeds of life, it is He who unceasingly nurtures and encourages growth. God invites and trusts us to play our part. We have the *'free will'* to choose what is best for our development and growth, and more than that, He, God has given each of us the gift of an Angel to call upon for help, for guidance and protection. It is our personal choice whether to believe so as to evolve into the very best specimen of life, we ever can be.

God invites us to accept and utilise the help and support of His messengers who eagerly wait to help. Angels bring help and support to human beings, animals, creatures and more as exemplified in Jimmy's experience.

'One day, you know one of those rare days when it wasn't raining. (laughing) I decided I would tackle the overgrown lawn. At the side garden there was a trail of small white feathers. Not many but enough to lead to something. Each one looked so new and each was spaced out about a foot apart. I followed the path and there under the overgrown braches of the hedge reaching out onto the grass, was a black bird.

The bird didn't resist as I reached down and lifted it up. Cupped in my hands I realised that the bird had been in the wars. Its left wing was sparsely dressed; when I spread the wing out, it was evident that there was nothing broken.

Its feathered wing was badly damaged. After cleaning what feathers were left, I prayed that this wee creature would be okay.

After stroking the little creature, the bird began to react. It began to show positive signs of pending recovery. The next day the black bird had gone and somehow I knew that something extraordinary had occurred. Two days later I left an apple out near the back door for the birds. Sometime later on I went out to go to the bin, and low and behold there it was, the black bird with the sparsely clothed wing.

I believe that the Angels led me to that helpless little creature in need of help'.

The fundamental notion that we can avail of some sort of healing energy from God is one thing, but the notion that an unseen and unheard spiritual being can bring about a sense of well-being is a difficult phenomenon for many people to consider.

Frequently, when faced with tragedy, illness or discord, one of the most common questions asked is *'Where is God?'*

Where is God?

Where is God when this goes wrong or that goes wrong? And how could God allow this to happen or that to happen? Yet, when all is well sometimes this God is redundant but when the tide turns, so too does the human need for support and answers. We crave for signs!

Yet, all too frequently, the signs are there, but we are just not alert enough to recognise such. Somewhere, somehow in the midst of uncertainty it seems natural to place the blame onto everything and/or everyone else—hence when searching for a sense of understanding, predictably the same question is asked over and over— *'Where is God?'*

Yet, God sends His Angels to help us. But, how do we respond to such an invitation? Do we dare to open our minds and hearts to claim that which is for one's best or do we allow the influence of other people to impede the liberty to *'be'*? There are no limits to the requests we can make of the Angels who excitedly wait for your/my call.

Can you permit yourself to humbly submit to such a concept?

God created Angels to guide and protect us. But, as we have been granted the great gift of *'free will'*, the Angels can't actively assist without an invitation to do so. Sometimes we are easily distracted from that which is available. When illness or tragedies challenge us, what do we do?

Generally, we go into auto pilot. We rant and rave. We blame everybody and everything. We don't know whether to laugh or to cry.

But most of us do ask *'Where is God?'*

We may say *'It's so unfair.'* Or *'Why me?'* As adults, when we observe little children suffer and become confused, withdrawn and afraid, we plead for God to show Himself, as we search for understanding and enlightenment. When a child is sick there is a spiral effect: the child is frightened, the parent/s is scared, members of the extended family are weary and feel useless and in many instances the initial human reaction is to ask *'Where is God?'*

In the simplest way and embodied within Christian teaching there is the potential to perceive such a question as to be *'flying in God's face'*. But in our basic humanity, the mystery may be difficult to perceive. However, the same can be applied when we consider how Jesus, the son of God, would respond to such a question. As Jesus was both human and Divine, (as a result of Him taking on the human existence so as to understand and save humanity), would it be fair to say that surely He above all would be able to relate to this question, not just as a question but rather a prayer, a request for some sense of enlightenment.

A similar concept may become apparent when people are confronted with bereavement, dysfunctional behaviour or emotional disharmony, relationship problems, irreconcilable situations distrust, fear, disputes, anger, depression and/or interpersonal intimidation.

Take a moment to reflect and take stock of life, life as it is, not as you believe it should be or could be. Recognising that where you are and what you are doing is *'real'* and is a powerful connection with reality. Allow yourself to become aware of all the good that surrounds you: family, friends, inspiring and influential people, the wisdom of adults who have experience of the winding journey of life and living. Accept where you are at; embrace the beauty that fills your space: nature, people, therapies and more. Appreciate your life and how all these wonderful people, places and therapies affect yourself development and growth.

Don't pre-empt what might happen, it may never happen. Don't waste valuable time on the *'what ifs and what buts'*! Consider if you can, where God fits into all of this . . . and how the Angels may help you along life's journey.

Hey!

Let's get real here!

Believe it or not, God does exist.

Angels wait patiently on your call.

Angels do exist.

Angels do exist.

Just as in all things you/we have the great gift of '*free choice*' to believe or not to believe. But, when the chips are down, it is then we can appreciate that the Trinitarian God, as in God the Father, Son and Holy Spirit, all three in one, who care. Somewhere in the cosmos, a higher power transcends love in abundance to us, their care! We are invited to call for help and support, the journey is as good as we make it. Some people may say, '*I can speak to God anywhere*'.

Yes, that may be so.

However, it is good to go that step further and experience the quiet peacefulness of a Church, participate in the coming together where we can all experience the '*Word*' of God and partake of the Eucharistic meal at the table of the Lord . . .

The Church is not just a building.

It's a haven where you can escape to when opportunities challenge you, when decisions have to be made, when it seems your back is up against the wall, where it appears there is no-one to listen to you, no-one understands you.

In today's world, there is so much conflict and contradiction that people struggle with the challenges of Church. Frequently, there is a need to blame anybody and everybody rather than taking responsibility for self.

You know, that's okay too!

Yet, we need to learn from such.

Therefore, we have to nurture and feed ourselves. If we need spiritual guidance, we can't wait for someone else to provide such from afar.

A young man, a pop celebrity, told an interviewer on the radio, *'I am not religious, but, I am Spiritual'*.

Now what's that all about?

Within such a statement there is a sense of contradiction: on one hand this person is claiming to be spiritual and disassociating himself from being religious, yet, *'religious'* and *'spiritual'* are one in the same.

Ironically, such indicates a dichotomy in kind, that point to the contemporary awareness that there is some higher power, spirit and/or force that is present despite the macho language shielding the reality within.

We are invited to believe and allow God through the work of the Angels to guard and protect us from danger. This can occur in a number of different ways.

Great support from the heavenly guides can come about as a result of listening to a great speaker, or to the words of a song; or finding a feather when in a time of need, receiving something quite unexpectedly, being greeted by smiling eyes or the touch of someone who cares and so much more.

When everything just drifts aimlessly by, we frequently bypass some of the most profound signs of faith, hope and love.

Traditionally, it was perceived by many that it was the remit of the Church to provide and prescribe some form of medicine for the soul. However, within the Roman Catholic tradition, Vatican II opened the flood gates of the Church to a greater participation of laity. A juncture in which religion was scrutinised by many not adequately educated in the profound teachings of Church. Hence, the old school of thought has been misplaced giving way to an almost shirking off of responsibility. Religion in some instances is replaced by the label of *'Spirituality'* which in essence is one in the same. Yet, for some people, it appears easier to say *'I am Spiritual'* rather than admit to being *'Religious'*, therefore, not admitting to a particular religious faith but indicative of believing in something.

In recent times, possibly as a result of negative press and human weaknesses, many people have turned away from Church for various reasons, directly or indirectly. Some people receive some sort of solace by *'pointing the finger'* so to speak or placing the blame of their negative approach to religion onto others.

But in reality there is little growth when we don't open ourselves to challenge. Yet, when in need, it is good to have someone to turn to! Frequently, when there is a tragedy or crisis there will always be those who will ask *'Where was God?'* or *'Where is God in all of this or that?'*

In basic humanity, there appears to be a need for explanations especially when a calamity, tragedy or a disaster occurs.

Not so long ago, Bridget's sister was diagnosed with a progressive cancer. The news brought with it a mix of reactions. The cancer victim was a married woman in her mid forties, her husband of twenty two years was angry, he was angry with God, with the doctors and with the world. Bridget's nieces and nephews all of whom were young adults couldn't equate why such a good loving mother should suffer.

Emotions ran riot. Some of the greatest anger came from younger members of the family. *'Why mummy, she never did anything except help everybody; she never said or did anything to hurt anybody. She always told me that God loves us! But, if somebody loves me, how could they hurt me? I just can't get my head around this',* Jamie said followed by an outcry from Jennifer who asked *'Aye! I agree with you Jamie, Where is God now then? Mummy was always so faithful to her belief in God, she wouldn't let us say a word about anyone, and now look at what he does.*

Aye! God . . .

Some reward, eh! Well come on then, how could God allow this to happen? You know, it's just not fair, I just can't understand either.'

Understandably, they couldn't figure out how God could be so cruel. As far as they were concerned, somebody they perceived to be so good, who cared and loved them, was given a death sentence. Bridget asked a local religious to counsel the young people.

Such a challenge, there were so many questions all with a common thread: words neatly woven together yet based in quest:

'Where is God?'

The outcome was powerfully enriching. The counsellor invited the young people to listen, to meditate and to rest in the spirit. Angel energy healing brought a quiet sense of tranquillity.

Another example of how such a question was answered revealed itself as Megan's ordinary everyday routine collided with an extraordinary happening. This story is unbelievable testimony of faith. *'I got up as usual. It was just another day. September 11, 2001—8.22a.m. As I was running late, I skipped breakfast and grabbed a snack bar from the press. Pulling on my coat, I remember seeing a brilliant flash of light. It seemed to swish past me as I opened the door. Before the door closed behind me I felt the presence of my Angel. (I always know my Angel is with me).*

I can't explain why I felt the way I did, I just thought there was a strange feeling as I walked in a running step to the far end of the block. On approaching the train station, there was some commotion. But, because I was late, I just blanked everything out, I ignored the announcements and pushed my way towards the platform as a train came roaring towards a stop. Oblivious to all going on, I got onto the train heading towards the Twin Towers at the World Trade Centre (WTC).

I got off the PATH train at the WTC; there was a strange smell, the air seemed heavier than usual. The further away I walked from the train the stronger the dreadful smell of something burning grew. As I turned the corner the smoke, Oh! My God, it was awful. There were emergency vehicles trying to make their way through paths now strewn with debris: fragments of stone and cement, sheets of printed material drifting along the pathways and occasionally lifting up into the haze beyond.

The tension was unbelievable. But, I kept walking across paths overloaded with rubble. As I stumbled my way towards a building on the corner of 1 WTC (north tower), the nearer I walked towards the WTC the more the smell and the haze of smoke became so heavy. So heavy, I could hardly see to make my way towards work.

All I could see as I scrambled through the thick smoke was mayhem. When I was near the World Financial Centre (WFC) a gentle voice kept saying 'turn left', but I ignored it until I could go no further. Everyone that could walk or run was going the other direction. It was as if everyone had become like robots. I began to cry. I had no idea what was going on. Tears were running down the faces of everyone whom I met. I tried to stop a man to ask what was going on, but he like everyone else didn't stop, but just pushed me aside.

The sense of urgency to get away was surreal; it was as if there was a human stampede. After being knocked to the ground not once or twice but repeatedly, I was crying so sorely, it was as if my heart would stop. I was scared and roared out like a lion: "Oh! God, am I going to die? Where are you? I am not ready to die, please help me?" Again, the voice told me to turn left. As I did, there under a small mountain of rubble I could see what I thought were two bright blue beads shining through. The eerie sight of shining beads of blue unnerved me so much so that I felt as if I should move on.

Then, I turned back.

As I pulled back the debris I could see a face, two blue eyes and a partial mask of dust and grit, and a heavy flow of tears creating unparallel murky streaks tipping awkwardly into the corners of a wide opened mouth.

My bare hands immediately became shovels. As I clawed to clear away the layers of stone and dirt, encasing an injured man, I was aware of a strong sense of inner strength.

Eventually, I reached out and tried to help to drag him out of the rubble. As I pulled the shattered body, I felt sick; he was heavy, blood stained and the smell of death scared me. I wanted to leave him there but couldn't!

I called out "God, where are you?"

Then all of a sudden there was a smell of gas and I began to panic. Again, I called out "God where are you? Please,

please help!' And 'out of the blue' a young man appeared and within seconds he had dragged the injured man to the corner of the street. I just sat down and nursed my head in my hands. When I became calm and raised my head, I witnessed the injured man being lifted by medical personnel but there was no sign of the man who had helped.

I have no idea whom I had helped that day and probably will never know. Likewise, I will never know the man who appeared and disappeared just as quickly, but, I believe, that in the midst of all the awful devastation God heard my plea and an Angel was sent to help.

Numbers associated with the day the WTC was destroyed are 9.11.2002.82—Angel numbers: 911, 200, 282, strongly connected with the Divine.

This last story points to the acceptance that God and the Angels were at hand. God was not responsible for the disaster, such was man-made but the important factor is that God was present not to *maim* but to *heal*. For some people that day, God's presence helped to sustain and free survivors and to help reveal bodies of the fatally wounded and the bodies of those who had died. The presence of God and His Angels has reignited the inner need for spiritual growth. We are encouraged to open ourselves to the belief that we have a responsibility to '*be*' and to claim that which is for one's highest good.

In more recent times it has become more apparent and accepted that the soul is an important and integral part of the wholeness of self and people have embraced the idea that they too, have a duty to work to make good.

The more we call upon the Angels, the more their energy becomes an apparent presence. The more we call upon the Angels, the more grace we receive; the more grace we receive the more we believe. Consequently, the more grace we receive, the greater the ability to embrace and hold firm to the concept that we are people worthy of God's love, support and guidance.

Thus, in time we realise that we are invited to call upon the Angels and to avail of the tools provided by God to help us through the journey of life and living!

God Provides the Tools!

Such a small word with so many definitions! Tools!

'Life is not a God 'ill fix it show'.

'Life is what you make it'.

God provides the tools?

There are so many tools available to help support and direct us unconditionally through life and living. It is up to each of us whether to avail of such help or not. It is easy to wade through life blaming everything and everybody for this, that and the other. We can swim with the tide or swim against the tide. When we swim with the tide it is obviously much easier, all seems more serene and affirming. On the other hand, we can choose to swim against the tide where problems consistently cause us to momentarily feel overpowered with the velocity of the life's demands.

God provides the tools; we are invited to put the varied and wide range of tools to good use. What is a tool?

A tool is an implement, a device, an instrument, basically a piece of equipment which is used to serve in various spheres of life and living. When one talks of an implement, it is assumed that such is applied or put into service as you do when needed, for self or to assist those in need. A device refers to a mechanism such as a domestic appliance or a work place boiler or other equipment necessary to produce something of value. Something as simple as a cooker which is beneficial to the provision of food; a washing machine which eases the workload associated with laundry, or a boiler or burner needed to efficiently heat a building. Whatever the applied label, each piece of equipment has a role to play; each has its own particular use, each appreciated by those in need!

In life and living there are so many tools to assist us through the daily journey to eternity. We have the responsibility to avail of all that is good to help make the various transitions needed whether for self or for others.

In contemporary society we have much on offer through the vein of technology. Through the use of computers we have world wide access by surfing the web. Within the domain of health there are so many interventions and varied approaches to enhance life. The Scriptures written so long ago have so many stories to tell that affirm us; and despite its longevity the 'WORD' is as meaningful today as it was when first written. It's just the language that may seem alien to some people but when read and digested, the food is full of nutrients and fibre more wholesome than humanity can comprehend.

Anne's story is an example of the power of a tool, in that of a message she received while watching a DVD, and how such was the catalyst to saving her life.

'My mum and sister lived in Liverpool, both terminally ill. My niece lived next door and was their main carer. Unfortunately my niece was also taken ill and needed to undergo treatment (chemo and radiotherapy but she doesn't like people knowing). When she discovered she was ill, she contacted the family, as we lived in different parts of the country and asked if we could all help a bit more with mum and my sister's care.

As I worked part-time I was able to travel up most weekends, sometimes if things were bad mid-week as well. The journey took 2hours on a good day, up the motorway. I had been doing the journey for several months and got myself into a routine. Finish work 3.30pm Friday, go home, pack, cup of tea, etc. then set off about 6 to miss the heavy traffic.

One Friday in October/November I worked all day but was aware that the back of my right leg, down from my knee was very tender. I mentioned it to my colleagues in passing and just carried on. I drove up the motorway and commenced my weekend of looking after mum and my sister. Nurses were popping in and out and one noticed I was limping slightly. I told her about my leg and she checked it for me. She advised me to go to the walk-in clinic but as it was over the other side of town I said I'd wait till I got home and see the doctor if it was still sore.

It was obvious that my mum and my sister appeared a lot worse than me! I drove home late on the Sunday night and went straight to bed. When the alarm went off, I got up but found I couldn't put any weight on my leg. The pain was awful. (This sounds dramatic, but I was laughing at the time!) I got out of bed and hopped to the stairs, sat on my bottom down to the hall and then crawled to the kitchen to make a cup of tea.

Meanwhile, my husband was asking what the matter was. When I told him and he realised I couldn't walk, even hopping was extremely painful, he decided to get me to the doctor.

At the doctors I was diagnosed with 'thrombophlebitis', [**Thrombophlebitis** is phlebitis (vein inflammation) related to a thrombus (blood clot.)] *I was sent home with painkillers and told if the back of my lower leg (calf) went hard to come back or go to the hospital. I was off work resting and keeping my leg elevated as advised but it didn't seem to be improving. The pain was controlled by the painkillers.*

Thursday arrived and things seemed much the same. It was early evening and I was home alone. I decided to watch a DVD. I looked through the choice and picked 'Angels and Demons' as every time I wanted to watch it I was outvoted.

I found the start really interesting—what happens when a Pope dies—as I had read about the protocol surrounding such an event and was impressed that it had been researched so well. As the film progressed I sat back and relaxed, getting into the storyline.

About 3/4 of the way through the lead character asks if any of the Cardinals who have been kidnapped are on medication. The priest replies yes. He says the Cardinal has to have daily injections because he has thrombophlebitis.

I rewound the DVD and listened again. I thought I'm having that and I'm only on painkillers. As the research seemed accurate at the start I began to think. I phoned my

Aunt who was a nurse; she reassured me but said that I should probably go to the hospital. When my husband came home, I asked him if, like me, he thought my calf felt hard. He did.

We went straight to the hospital.

*The triage nurse sent us to the doctor immediately after she checked me (about 5mins wait in all). They tested my blood, checked my leg and decided to give me an injection in my stomach. The doctor said it looked like a DVT [***Deep vein thrombosis***] *and that the injection would stop the blood clot from breaking up. Keeping me safe was now paramount. My blood sample was sent to the DVT clinic and if the doctor's diagnosis was correct I would be contacted the next morning.*

The clinic opens at 8.30am.

I was contacted at 8.32am and told to come in a.s.a.p. I was there by 8.50am. I was sent for an ultra sound scan. It seems I had a massive blood clot in my right leg! The nurses couldn't believe that I hadn't been referred on the Monday and said it was surprising that parts of it hadn't broken away . . . . and I was very lucky, someone had been watching over me!

I had a week of injections into my stomach and then 6mths on 'Warfarin.' I am off the medication but if I wish to fly long haul, I have to have injections before I fly and when I land. I also have to be aware of any pains in my leg as I am at higher risk of getting another DVT.

I do believe angels were watching over me. I had other opportunities to watch that DVD when I was alone but wasn't in the mood, and when the family were home, wouldn't let me. It was as if it was kept for this moment.'

As in the case of Anne's experience, a friend of mine who was having difficulty with her niece, who had lost her mum, found Angelic guidance in the form of a story about a young girl's internal and personal struggle, with the loss of her mother and her transition into adolescence. The story portrayed in a DVD entitled *'Daddy's little Angel'*, allowed her to identify with her niece Molly's inner struggle.

'Molly was a typical happy go lucky child. As she approached her twelfth birthday her mum fell ill. Day by day she was there watching her mum grow frail. Within a really short time her mum died. Molly's struggle was enormous. In one way Molly was aware that her mum was dying, yet, on the other hand she didn't want to lose her. For months after her mum's death, Molly spent hours away in her own room. She was hard to work with and her transition into adolescence was laced with deep anger. She felt victimised at school because of her plain and sometimes unfeminine, almost macho image and subsequent behaviour.

As Molly's aunt and temporary guardian, I was getting frustrated. I was a breaking point!

She wouldn't speak to me.

She wouldn't confide in anyone but I knew she was in a terrible place. Her dad worked abroad and was due back within months to work permanently near home.

In some ways she seemed to resent everyone and everything. She felt abandoned even though she knew her dad was coming home for good. I spoke to Kate and she suggested that I might get Molly to watch a DVD called 'Daddy's little Angel', portraying a story relevant to my niece's sense of inner struggle. I was willing to try anything. I believed that if I could get her to watch the DVD, she might open up.

She was in her daily snappy mood but said she would humour me! Who was humouring who? Every excuse under the sun distracted her as we tried to settle down to view the DVD.

I waited.

Then, finally she sat down beside me.

Well, believe it or not!

It worked, after about the tenth time of asking her to watch the DVD. The story meant so much to her. As the story unfolded, she moved closer to me and nestled close to me on the sofa. As she silently cried I wiped away her warm rears. She even said "I could feel the pain that wee girl had" and she hugged me. As the film was drawing to a close, as if planned, her dad had quietly come into the living room and tapping her on the shoulder she gasped and leapt up to hug him. Such a wonderful moment!

One of those bitter sweet moments in time!

She cried, he cried and I cried.

There is little doubt that if we are open to share our pain and listen, there is always help at hand. The Angels gave Kate a tool to help us through a horrendous time of uncertainty based in hope, ultimately grounded in deep love.'

Cheryl exclaimed with a deep sigh that the DVD was an instrument of support and profound enlightenment.

Affirmation is a powerful tool which emanates from the pool of positivity that provides us with the feeling of hope. Such encompasses a sense of worth, of belonging and wholeness. Positivity and all associated with such outweigh the negativities that lurk and seek attention.

An instrument is that which is used in various approaches, in which to repair, rebuild or to restore that in need. Within the field of music an instrument is that which is used to produce and render melodious sounds to others. Within an orchestra, there are a wide range of instruments used to perform the best possible rendition of music to the world. In the hands of a tattooist or an artist, an implement, a device, may be use to create something awesome, beautiful and inspirational. Afterall, beauty is in the eye of the beholder. We smile when we see images which portray us, some very flattering and serene images and indeed some caricatures exhibiting a more worldlier view of the Angelic realm. Images transform our thinking. If a serene image of an Angel is found we automatically think good, positive and content.

However, if confronted with an image portraying evil, we may become ill at ease, negative and uncertain. Occasionally, it is envisaged that something which appears positive to one person, may be negative to another and vice versa. There are no rules; it is all about personal choice. Such is exemplified through two individual experiences. Jonah and Nora were both given two pictures to study for ten minutes. Then they were instructed: *'Turn the first picture upright and turn the other face down. Now, write down ten words which describe the picture before you.'*

Looking at the list of ten words it was obvious that this first picture was of a positive nature. Words such as nice, attractive, beautiful, serene and lovely were recorded by both.

Then they were both asked to place that picture away and to turn up the second picture. Again they were instructed: *'Write down ten words which describe this image.'* In doing so the outcome was not as transparent. Jonah perceived this picture to be as inspiring and attractive as the other. While, Nora believed the second image to be negative and disturbing and recorded words such as awful, scary, dark and dismal. The experiment revealed how the tool of thought permits the uniqueness of individual thinking and beliefs of another to be explored and respected.

'Tools' simply refers to *'that opening onto life'*. A tool is an implement of service. A tool can be that of a tangible or intangible nature, that which is seen or heard; such can be a hammer, a screwdriver, a pen, a brush, a telephone, a television, an MP3 player, a game, a book, a needle, a pin or something which is vocal, a word or a sound, indeed even the affirmation of another.

Tools are to be used, not abused.

God gives us the tools.

Tools are not to be used in a destructive way, to break down that which is not broken. We are encouraged to use the tools we receive to build up and to enhance life and living. God gives us the *'free will'* as to how we employ such equipment for the rebuilding, repairing and regeneration of self. Likewise, Angels are the unseen, unheard tools and we have the choice to believe whether they exist or not!

Many confirm that continuing signs and symbols indicate the belief that *'Angels do exist.'*

Angels do exist!

While the Church is indeed the most blessed and sacred place, external visions, apparitions, spiritual encounters may occur. Sometimes there are happenings and encounters which take place and have little meaning at that initial moment. However, all is revealed in time. When God believes it is appropriate, the meaning of such will be made known to you, me, and whoever!

An Angel is one whom God has sent to help us achieve love, happiness and peace while on this planet. We are not sent here to suffer, we are sent here to do the best we can with the time and the tools available to us. God has given us all the gift of '*free-will*'; it is our personal choice to believe, and to call and to appreciate what God has designed to be our spiritual aides.

The image of an Angel is personal. For some the Angel may have a divine appearance with the most beautiful feathered wings ever imaginable; a human being radiating love and happiness, or a faceless non-gender figure. For other people an Angel may not have a definitive appearance and the idea of wings may not be considered. Either way, the important thing to remember, is that the Angel is the gift God has given. This unseen, unheard being of the heavenly sphere will guide and protect and will swiftly respond. This messenger of God will endeavour to do all within his/her power to bring about that which is ultimately for one's highest good.

In embracing and accepting the gift of the Angels, the healing power of the Angels and the love of God brought about by the Angels, it is also important to note and understand 'Angels', their function and role in bringing about ultimate joy, love and peace into our hearts which in turn will benefit all. Such will help to make the world a much better place for everyone and everything. Therefore, the opportunity will focus on the acknowledgement to be aware that Angels do exist; accept their contribution to humanity and appreciate the activity of God's messengers who serve to please. In so doing we will experience the work of the Angels and how we work with Angels.

Quite often it is at a later moment, minutes, hours, days and more before the significance of the message is revealed, as exemplified in a story shared with a young lad from Carrick.

Jamie said *'I sat by the river bank with my collie dog, Rex. As I gazed out onto the water I thought I saw a fish jump up, I looked again and as sure as I was sitting there, the fish jumped up again and added a further invitation by springing up out of the water a few times with the inclusion of a display of flips and twists.*

The display was so wonderful, yet, strange.

I thought it was my imagination, but the more the scene evolved the more Rex ran towards the water barking in a playful kind of way.

I was sitting thinking to myself was this for real? . . .

As I left the riverside and walked almost in a trance towards home, I deliberated how I could tell anyone about what I had seen. I could almost imagine my parent's reaction and there's no doubt my friends would have thought I was off my rocker'. After a long drawn out pause Jamie continued, *'As I turned the corner and made my way towards the door, I was surprised . . . there were many people in the house. Rather confused and bewildered I cautiously entered the room. Maura, a close family friend took me aside and explained that my dad had had a serious accident at work. I was so relieved, I thought he was dead. She continued to explain that at work, my dad got his leg caught up in a shaft and there was a fear that he might have to lose a leg.*

God, I remember sobbing so sorely, that I thought my heart would burst as I sat alone in the corner of the kitchen. Eventually my mum, Anna, appeared and immediately came over and hugged me, she hugged me that hard I could hardly breathe as she nestled me to her breasts. When she released me, I could sense she was quite calm even though a trickle of tears rolled down her face which had damped my face.

As she lifted my head, she looked into my face and she told me that she wasn't afraid and everything would be fine and explained: 'Cause earlier in the morning I thought I saw an Angel, no I know I saw an Angel at the far end of the garden where the statue of the Blessed Virgin is housed'. I thought if mum can share that with me, then I tell her about his experience.

After sharing together, we just sat quietly and embraced each other as we waited on the phone to ring. As we waited the local priest, Fr. P called at the house. After the update as regards the accident, we told Fr. P about our earlier experiences, he didn't flinch, he just sat and listened. When we finished telling our stories, Fr. P asked if there was a Bible in the house. Flicking through the pages, Fr. P opened it at the 'Book of Tobit, 6:2', and read out the following: 'The boy left with the Angel and the dog followed behind . . . . the boy had gone down to the river to wash his feet, when a great fish leapt out of the water and all but swallowed his foot'.

According to Jamie, it appears that as those in the room listened to Fr. P; there was an instant sense of awe. It was as if the reading was saying that everything would work out. The link between the passage read by Fr. P and what had happened to Jamie's father, the Angel whom Anna believed she had seen and the scenario played out by the fish that had entertained Jamie, powerfully presented a profound message of hope!

'Somehow, there was an acceptance that my dad was protected and all would be well. I can still hear the telephone ringing . . . everyone sat in total silence, a silence mixed with fear and hope, sheer excitement willing good news. Fr. P got up and embraced my mum as she re-entered the room. After a few deep breaths and a deliberate pause, she declared that all was well, my daddy wasn't to lose his leg and he was peacefully sleeping in recovery. There was an unexplainable silence, followed by a thunderous outburst of joy', Jamie concluded.

The Angels were present within this whole story and Jamie has never forgotten the day the *'Angel'* and the fish brought a message later to be revealed as he recollected on his experience: *"Frequently, I have thought about that day and how everything worked out so well. I now share that story with my children and they too believe in Angels. When I go with the children down by the riverside, I reflect on the Scriptural message read out to us by Fr. P.*

Who knows what might have been without the words of hope which gave such comfort in a time of uncertainty . . . I know Angels do exist!"

Within life and living there is a great need for signs, we search for affirmation. Angels are ready to help; just call is an invitation to everyone.

On August 15, 1998, without warning, a car bomb exploded in Omagh, a town in the Northern Ireland. There were many casualties and 31 innocent people were killed, 2 of which were unborn twin babies. Despite the troubled times leading up to this atrocity, this horrific incident may now be seen as the catalyst to Peace. Frequently, we encounter nudges from the higher spheres as revealed in following story in which Maggs had an immediate thought to call upon the Angels, as she feared for her safety and that of her children. Maggs had gone to Omagh that day to buy school uniforms for her children and relates her memory of that day.

'Megan was in the buggy. Jason, Jenny and Martin were straddling along behind me. We made our way through the Arcade and as we turned to make our way to Watterson's in the High Street, the Police appeared in what seemed to be more than usual numbers. I had a strange feeling and my stomach was shaking.

Because of living through the Troubles, we continued on, passing Boots and heading for Watterson's'. When I think back on it now, I remember there was a strange, kinda eerie atmosphere despite the fact that weather wise it was a lovely summer day. Isn't hindsight great?' she nervously continued.

After a long pause, Maggs was anxious to tell more of her experience: *'When we went into the shop, there was a lot of confusion. The shop assistants were fussing about trying to steer customers back out onto the street. It was awful; nobody knew what was going on. When I think back now, it seemed the staff weren't even sure why they were doing what they were doing!*

Everybody was shouting.

It was crazy!

As we came out of Watterson's, we were about to go into 'Boots' when a man with outstretched arms pushed us towards the Arcade. By that stage there were people running in all directions. It was total mayhem. I was getting really panicky and I was roaring at the 'wains'; they weren't running fast enough. I tripped, the buggy fell over and Jamie, Jenny and Martin were all squealing. As I got to my feet and reached to lift Megan, there was the most unmerciful bang. Within an instant a cloud of smoke travelled over the whole area and little pieces of grit showered us. My immediate reaction was to run. I could feel something piercing into my side. I fell. As the pain increased I was aware that I was bleeding . . . . with great difficulty, I cried out "Angels, please help me. Help us get out of this".

As quick as I called upon the Angels, help was at hand. A nurse and a doctor took me by the hand and sat me down on the ground. The open wound in my side was treated and myself and the children were put into an Ambulance and taken to the County Hospital. Since that day, I have never had any doubt about the existence of Angels and believe that God sent his messengers to bring love and Peace into this unexpected and surreal situation. With my belief in God and His Angels I and my family are spiritually free!'

Sacred codes confront us daily. In reality happenings and contradictions exist. We are challenged to trust and call upon the Angels in time of need. We have the responsibility to decipher right from wrong and to make the ultimate choice for wellness of self.

It is easy to allow yourself to be deluded by external influences, to do something despite the inner voice in your mind that shouts out not to do so, thus exhibiting paradoxes of life that tease.

Life's Paradoxes

Even in what is perceived to be the best situations, even believe it or not, in the most Christian or non-religious basis, decisions have to be made within the depth of truthfulness. One thing we can strive for is the perfection of imperfection . . . .

In the real sense of perfection it is not a possible goal, yet, there is the reality that imperfection is profoundly possible. Much of what we encounter is flawed to some extent . . . therefore, perfection as an entity is possible if applied to the realisation that perfection of imperfection is undoubtedly a reality.

All too frequently, truth is masked whether it is as a result of fear, unease, vulnerability, apprehension and/ or embarrassment. In today's society there is a greater awareness of personal responsibility and accountability for one's life and living. Abuse is no longer tolerated. Everyone is entitled to live life to the optimum.

Human beings are blessed individuals worthy of the respect to make intelligent and appropriate decisions.

Everyone is encouraged to make decisions not influenced by others but based on personal beliefs. So often external factors influence the way people react and make choices.

Sometimes situations may arise where decisions have to be made, but for some reason or another there is a void in which the choice becomes complicated. So much so, that what is right is staring clearly in front of you, yet, for some reason whether as a consequence of others' reactions or behaviour, an alternative outcome emerges. What seems so easy can actually be so difficult. On the one hand, it is easy to know what the proper choice should be, but on the other hand there is a need to please or succumb to the beliefs of others.

Various contemporary therapies, alternative and/ or complementary: Angelology, psychology, theology, counselling, meditation, yoga and various fitness programmes offer so much to the wellbeing of humanity. But dare we believe and avail of such or do we become hindered by the perceptions of others.

One of the biggest problems we are faced with is the difference between '*free will, free choice and rules and regulations*' as set out by those in authority, whether it be State or Church or otherwise. There can be difficulties with the simplicity of words, right/wrong; yes/no; love/ hate; can/can't; do/don't and so on.

Sometimes the contradiction between '*love*' and '*hate*' can be underestimated. We may very well believe that we hate someone but somewhere deep within there is another force at work indicative of love.

I can hear you say, '*How could this be?*'

In actual fact it's quite probable that what is considered as *hate* may profoundly mask *real love*. Such may occur for various reasons.

Take Anna's story and consider her dilemma. *'I met my husband when I was at secondary school. In our early teens we were inseparable. We went everywhere together. We were in LOVE! Before my sixteenth birthday, I became pregnant and in our day that was the most awful shameful thing to happen. We were marched up to the parochial house.*

(There was little in the line of pep talks back then).

It was a case of being read the riot act. Arranging a date for marriage and sent off to be parents. But sure we were on cloud nine, we were in LOVE. It wasn't long before the honeymoon was over and reality took its toll.

So much changed as the years rolled by and real life had to be lived. The fairy tale had come to an abrupt end. There was resentment on both parts. Frequently we both felt trapped.

We argued.

We fought.

And eventually we believed we HATED each other. We couldn't be in the same room without fighting. We continually blamed each other for not being able to do this, that or the other. When we looked for help we were told 'You made your bed now lie in it'. After fifteen years neither of us could take it anymore. We had two children and they suffered when we argued and fought, so it was agreed that we would go our separate ways.

I took the children.

We stayed in the house and the man I adored moved into a place of his own outside of the town.

But, night after night I cried myself to sleep. I couldn't understand why things didn't work out for us . . . sure we were so in LOVE. How could such love turn into such hatred? The struggle got worse. I took an overdose, not once, not twice but three times.

Not knowing what to do and with no family support I went along to the parochial house where I considered our future was decided. But, now two decades on, there wasn't only a new priest but a spiritual person with a new approach towards the wellbeing of people in need. After a long series of meetings, it was agreed that my then estranged husband and I could begin to talk things out. The underlying belief that we just 'hated' each other was the first hurdle.

(laughing)

I remember when we first met in the reception room at the parochial house after years apart, my knees were shaking, I had butterflies in my tummy and I broke out in a cold sweat. It was just like the way I reacted when we first met as teenagers.

This reaction made me very nervous.

But, the facilitator (the priest) was not a dictator but a man of compassion, understanding and humanity. As a consequence the LOVE that we had for each was timidly reignited and the confusion between 'Love and Hate' was explained and teased out so well that in time we were reunited and are inseparable today. All through the journey of confusion I was so comforted when I prayed. Occasionally a feather would fall at my feet and I knew that God and His Holy Angels were protecting me and the children.

Now to top it all, they even helped to bring us back together as a family. The new priest was an Angel, that's for sure!'

So do we dare to ask, *'Whose life is it, anyway?'*

Why should anyone yield to the power of the other?

Why should we allow the contradictions associated with the simple words *'yes'* and/or *'no'* to determine how life is lived, or how choices are made?

Why should we leave ourselves open to the transference of others?

In its simplest form, it seems fair to suggest that we want not only to be taught that we have *'free will'* but rather to believe that we have *'free will'*. But, despite the basic understanding that we are free to choose, there are in reality many contradictions. We are constantly at odds with what we can do and what we can't. Yet, the basic message is that such can work when based on good judgement and common sense.

St. Augustine's approach to the *"free choice of the will"* supposes that *"there can be no denying that we have a will."* The Catechism of the Catholic Church echoes this, saying, *"Endowed with a spiritual soul, with intellect and with free will, the human person is from his very conception ordered to God and destined for eternal beatitude."* (1711).

It has been suggested that when people are ruled by feelings, emotions, and the inner guilt associated with feeling the need to do everything, look out for everyone, such has the potential to diminish the dignity of a person. The weight of the pain and emotional dysfunction becomes a burden and in time imbalance if not attended to, may manifest itself in a form of illness.

The body, soul and/or mind may become lethargic, restless or die. All too often it is the ego that is in the driving seat, as in reality no-one can live the life of/or for another fellow human being. Consequently, we empower external factors to dictate life and living. We fear to say *'no'* when we really mean *'no'* and to say *'yes'* when we really mean *'yes'*. Using the analogy of a ball, consider that all too often we unwittingly permit ourselves to become a human ball, where we are indirectly and unintentionally kicked about, thrown about and quite often there is no-one there to catch us as we fall.

We lack the courage to *'be'*.

We silently cry when we really want or know that it is appropriate to say *'no'* but we say *'yes'* and vice versa. Ironically, when we are afraid that we are hurting or letting someone down, we are in actual fact, wounding and stunting personal growth. At this juncture we are enveloping ourselves in a cloak of false security, 'cause other people are not privy to the inner struggle being played out. Dispose of the costume and the mask and allow yourself to be loved, appreciated and employ the gift of *'free will/personal choice'* with no conditions attached.

Protected and reinforced with the gift of *'free will'*, we are duty bound to make decisions based on a well-formed conscience determining what is good and evil. No-one wants to make an ill-informed decision. Generally, we all want what is best for ourselves and those whom we encounter. Likewise, for those who embrace the concept of Angels and the power of God's messengers, there is always guidance and protection in abundance.

Sometimes we can be blind and deaf in relation to the ministering spirits of God. Life can be so confusing, contradictory and demanding that it is easy to become lethargic and desolate. Occasionally, something unexpected can bring the light back into the dimming world of aloneness, isolation, estrangement and so on.

But isn't it true that very often we make decisions based on what others might think or say.

Just a wee reminder: *'Whose life is it, anyway?'*

Allison shared this story when discussing the power of the Angels and the influence of others with regard to decision making. *I don't know why, but for some reason I was fascinated by the idea of Angels. To some of my friends the concept of Angels was nonsense. So, for a long time I was so empowered by them and their perceptions in relation to such a subject, that I denied myself the great spiritual support I had longed for. Every so often, the notion came into my head but I was quickly reminded not to go there.*

However, one day when I was badly hurt, I could hear a voice reassuring me that everything would be alright. I thought I was going crazy,

I was hearing voices!

But, the quiet gentle voice persisted.

I realised at that point that there was someone looking after me. I could feel the presence of someone near. As the day went on there was a great peace all around. The sun seemed to fully break through the sky and the light swept through the house. There was light and heat surrounding me like I had not experienced for such a long time.

Unexpectedly, there was a knock at the door which disrupted what was beginning to be a very peaceful time.

On approaching the door, I could see the shadow of what I believed to be a woman. As I opened the door, to my surprise there was a woman whom I hadn't seen for years. Standing there holding a spray of flowers and a package in her hand.

I stood and stared in disbelief.

I apologised for my shocked reaction and invited her in. As we talked and caught up on all that happened in the intervening years we celebrated with a cuppa. As we sat at the table, I awkwardly began to unwrap, the package.

I was aghast.

The little figure was that of an Angel. The little card simply read: Angel of Protection.

I was speechless.

Initially, overwhelmed, tears ran down my cheeks, I gasped. After telling my long lost friend about my belief in the Angels and how I allowed the influence of others to dissuade me from opening up to the world of Angels, I hugged her and thanked her.

It was at this juncture that I realised that I had for too long allowed external factors and influences of others to determine how I lived my own life. For too long, my life was dictated by everybody and everything, other than myself.

As I gazed at the little figure of an Angel, I immediately realised that I had received a sign. I knew that the Angels were looking after me. Since then I have read extensively and attended courses about Angels.

I have collected books about Angels.

I have Angel cards.

I no longer worry about what others think of me and my profound interest and belief in Angels. I have been granted *the great gift of believing in myself, regaining a sense of self worth and the belief that the Angels are with me always.'*

It is important, however, to respect the fact that there are those who do not believe or aspire to open to the concept that God exists and Angels exist. That's okay, that's cool!

Choice is yours! Choice is mine!

One of the greatest gifts we can afford to another is that of profound respect. Not everyone has the same level of faith as another. Faith is a personal response to openness of heart and soul. Indeed, more often than not, we may hear people say I am not religious but I am spiritual. Yet, when the chips are down, we all need something to hold on to as exemplified in the lyrics of *'Breakeven'* sung by the rock band, *'The Script'*, in which the opening lines read: *'I'm still alive but I'm barely breathing, Just praying to a God that I don't believe in . . .'*

Similarly, in the lyrics of *'If I die before you wake'* by Dustin Evans, there is an invitation to remember that everything is in the hands of God and that all *'We Need Is A Little Faith and Trust.'* Contemporary music is reflective of a society struggling to unveil the spirit of God at a time when it is not cool to *'be'* religious.

'Black Eyed Peas' in a song entitled *'Karma'* reminds us that *'What goes around, comes around,'* and that *'God is watching you and everything that you do'* and that *'I'ma leave it up to God what he got for you, I'ma leave it up to God what he got for me'*.

In another song *'God is a Girl'* sung *by 'Black Eyed Peas'* we are challenged to believe and perceive that *'God is a girl, She's only a girl, Do you believe it, can you receive it?'*

To some people the ideology may be controversial but in reality it is the existence of God which is the pivotal message with the invitation to recognise that we all have a vital role to play in His world.

Within the lyrics of Kate Bush's song: *'If I only could, I'd be running up that hill'* there is an invitation to consider that when hurt and pain are present, it is then that *'I'd make a deal with God, and I'd get him to swap our places.'* In a song by Adele called *'One and Only',* again, God is referred to in an affirmative way that *'God only knows, why it's taken me so long'.*

Sarah McLachlan's song, *'In the arms of an Angel',* is reflective of struggle and eventual comfort. It is reasonable to suggest that this song is about being insecure and anxious. Yet, it points to the realisation that with hope and faith, in time one can experience a deep sense of serenity.

When this song is rendered at a memorial service, the notion of the departed being in the arms of the Angels is a comforting image; such considers that the deceased is now free from the weight of the worldly demands and burdens on body, soul and mind. Peace is found in the notion that an Angel is accompanying the deceased into Eternity where time is without end.

In the contemporary world of music the list is endless in which we are challenged to open our hearts and our minds so as to receive that which is there to affirm and empower us.

When the lyrics of such contemporary songs are listened to with profound concentration, it is apparent that in a society in which God has, for many people, been placed out of sight, there is a deep search going on for Him.

Somewhere in the multifaceted, somewhat complicated and paradoxical experiences of today's world, is it fair to suggest, that there is a underlying albeit covert realisation that God does exist and that at some point, we can avail of calling upon the higher power for help and support.

We are reassured that as God is timeless, the eternal home we hope to reside in, is indeed, a place of serenity and ultimate calmness. Scripture invites us to consider a further dimension of time within a human concept depicting the dichotomies of time as outlined in Ecclesiastes 3: *"A Time for everything and a season for every activity under the heavens: a time to be born and a time to die, a time to plant and a time to uproot, a time to kill and a time to heal, a time to tear down and a time to build, a time to weep and a time to laugh, a time to mourn and a time to dance, a time to scatter stones and a time to gather them, a time to embrace and a time to refrain from embracing, a time to search and a time to give up, a time to keep and a time to throw away, a time to tear and a time to mend, a time to be silent and a time to speak, a time to love and a time to hate, a time for war and a time for peace"*. Therefore, within humanity we are not strangers to diversity and challenge.

So to whom can we turn to when we are in need? To God and the Angels, there is nothing too big or too small, just trust. It is the experiences of life and living which consolidate God's blueprint for one's life.

Ultimately, *'life's jigsaw puzzle'* is demanding and challenging but with faith, hope and love all pieces will eventually fall into place.

Life's Jigsaw Puzzle

Our lives are rather like a covert jigsaw puzzle. Each jigsaw piece designed and cut out by God's own hand. This analogy hopefully can illustrate the construction of the mystery of life and living. As we are unique in our design and abilities, the development of the final image will be undertaken in various ways, each individual piece will eventually have to fit into place. The important thing to remember is that frequently pieces will vie for attention as we endeavour to position the misplaced pieces appropriately.

Angels wait to hear the call for help. Answers may not come instantly but what is certain is that, that which is for one's highest good will emerge! We are invited to trust.

A big ask one may say!

In basic humanness it can be quite difficult to surrender to a God we cannot see or to believe that His heavenly aides await to respond to the needs of those who call!

So too, it is quite a challenge to comprehend that life is a personal mission. If we don't have an image or a blueprint, then how do we begin to solve a puzzle containing jigsaw pieces each owning their unique shape and size? Have you ever taken on a giant jigsaw puzzle and when near completion there are some pieces missing, frustrations mount.

Marlene's contribution to this chapter shows how relationships fit or don't fit into place.

'When I was turning eighteen, I really believed that I was in love. My world could never be complete without Danny. Every time we met my knees knocked, I shook inside and it all seemed so right. We were meant to be together. Danny was in the army and redeployed from Kettering to a post overseas, just three months after our wedding.

I thought my world was coming to an end. Six months passed and Danny arrived home. It was like we were just getting to know each other again. Very soon after his return home, I became pregnant with our first child and subsequently, our only child.

Another piece of the jigsaw puzzle slotted neatly into place. During the pregnancy there was a sense of ill ease growing between Danny and me. But, this was soon transformed into a wonderful time with the arrival of baby Chloe.

Life was wonderful.

Then, the dreadful day the 'Troubles' broke out in Northern Ireland was to be a pivotal moment that changed our beautiful peaceful world. Within the next year, Danny waited for his turn to be redeployed in Belfast. That day came all too soon. Chloe and I accompanied Danny to the station. If life is a jigsaw, then it is obvious that there are pieces which we receive that fit in and there are definitely pieces which just don't fit into creating the complete picture.

Months apart had a detrimental effect on my nerves. Every time I watched the News, I waited to hear of Danny being killed. Every time the post came, I was scared there would be no letter from him. Then one day, that awful day which is imprinted forever in my mind, a military vehicle stopped outside the house. Two uniformed officers came towards the door.

The door bell rang but I just couldn't move. I was stuck solid to the floor. I knew that to have military call to the house, such could only mean one thing. 'DEATH'

The personnel knocked on my neighbour's door and it was she who came in by my back door and opened the front door to such unwanted guests. I knew why they called but I have no idea to this day what they said, I heard nothing, nothing, not a word. I apparently just stood speechless and shocked.

Much of my life for the next few years remains a total blank to me. Chloe was looked after by my parents as I spent time in and out of a Mental Institution. Many pieces of my life's jigsaw are missing and I often wonder how life can ever be fully lived now that I have lost a vital corner piece of my life!'

Marlene's story epitomises the unwarranted experiences which challenge for space in the jigsaw of life. From birth to death, the challenge to choose the relevant pieces needed to complete life's journey are frequently marred intermittently with misplaced and covert pieces, seemingly alluring and seeking attention. Negative influences, illness and tragedies occasionally fracture life's structure continually developing. The frame may appear in fine fettle but it is what lies behind the exterior that fights for attention.

So can you imagine when a child is born, the perfect body houses thousands of interrelating parts, all of which make up the jigsaw of humanity? Through time some of the experiences and encounters of life and living, are jigsaw pieces which must be placed piece by piece to create the final picture. But as unlike a boxed jigsaw, there is no illustration or image to guide when trying to fit the pieces of your personal story into place. The process will vary from person to person. Some pieces may slot together easily with little effort involved, while occasionally some pieces may create conflict and prove to be complex in nature. The ultimate picture will not be complete until the final day arrives when the Creator will see the final piece put into place. Psalm 139:16 and Matthew 10:29-30 remind us that the days of our lives, have been predetermined by God. Therefore, the number of jigsaw pieces of each puzzle will differ from person to person.

The illustration is that God is advising us that unless you start correctly with the correct corner pieces as set out in Ephesians 2:20, any attempts to create the boundaries with the hope of completing the jigsaw puzzle of life will be pointless if the boundary or frame is fractured.

The Word of God should infuse the outer frame and the inner pieces of our jigsaw, thus, serving body, soul and mind. When we work to fill the spaces of life's jigsaw, we need to believe that the Creator, God, will help us identify the proper pieces which will fit together, and how to manage the pieces which don't fit into life's puzzle. At such times the invitation is to allow God and the Angels to help, to guide and support you.

Generally it is agreed that to try to put a jigsaw together the first thing we do is to search out the corner pieces akin to the foundation stones of a building, person! Followed by the straight edges of the bottom, top and two sides! Hence, the frame is complete. At the outset one missing piece of the frame creates a pivotal imbalance.

When a child is born, the first part of the jigsaw is put into place, followed by the corner pieces reflective of all family and friends who help to mould this new individual. As the child is baptized and begins to grow and develop, the straight edges are fixed together, piece by piece to create the outer picture of being.

Through education, the sacraments and interaction within society, the inner parts of the picture evolve. However, placing the pieces together won't always slot easily into place, as life and living undoubtedly will demand us to work to choose appropriate pieces to fit together and to identify those pieces which are not belonging to the evolving jigsaw!

From time to time, happenings and encounters in our lives have a tendency to provoke and challenge us.

Life's path is never straight.

Life's journey would lack energy if there were *'no ups and downs'* and/or *'ifs and buts'*!

As God knows how the final picture will appear, he also knows how such will emerge. But as we are the recipients of *'free will/free choice'* we are afforded the respectful mission to solve the jigsaw of one's life and living.

Life's puzzle will be finished irrespective of how we proceed. Though we are not privy to how the final picture will come together, we can be sure that just like there are a limited number of pieces in any jigsaw puzzle, such is mirrored by the number of days in one's life. Life will not and cannot go on forever. Therefore, when the pieces of life's puzzle run out, death embraces the final piece in which God's creation becomes fully picture perfect.

'I remember when my daddy was dying; a neighbour was reciting prayers and asking God to take my daddy home. At a young age, it seemed the most awful thing in the world. I was angry. At that moment in time I was struggling to believe that God would not heal my daddy and let him live. I had little understanding of the realities of life. But, the memory of that woman asking God to take my daddy to his eternal home haunted me for years. It wasn't until I grew into adulthood and found God again that I could begin to forgive myself for disliking my neighbour and to appreciate the pure intention of that woman praying to free my daddy from physical torture'.

It is a challenge to understand the good that comes with death. For Christians we are afforded the great invitation to believe that there is a better place awaiting us, a place of eternal tranquillity from which our parents one day will come to bring us home. With such in mind, death no longer holds or imprisons any of us in fear but rather bound in the hope that God will bring departed family and Angels to Himself.

'It took a long time to understand that my daddy's jigsaw puzzle was finally completed. The entire picture had come together. The pieces had all been put into place, there was no

room left for more. It was time! It was only lately that I could imagine the picture my daddy had acquired. Somewhere, deep within, I felt proud that I was part of that jigsaw puzzle of life as my daddy is within mine'. It's like a whirlpool. The jigsaw puzzles of life ripple out into society and in turn relevant pieces fit neatly together. In life as in death, with the power of God and the Angelic whispers, we surrender.

At this final part of our earthly journey, the Angels who accompany and guide us, will celebrate with the one entering eternal life. Therefore, it is the perfection of imperfection, which we strive to obtain that will yield God's final embrace. In the realisation that God will place the final piece in the jigsaw of life, we surrender to live in faith, hope and love.

While we wait for that moment, and endure the challenges that we encounter, we may indeed cry out, *'Turn to whom?'*

Turn to whom?

Who can we turn to when those around us can't even begin to comprehend what belies a change in behaviour, negative thought patterns and the darkness that no human eye can see? Within the place where the lights have grown dim or have gone out, the question is not just to turn to someone for help but for the guidance to the question, *'Turn to whom?'* It is difficult when in a confused state of mind, to think clearly enough to believe that there is help available. When a sense of hopelessness tries to drive you, don't panic.

Aye, aye!

'Easy for you to say', I can hear you say, almost in a growing chorus of disbelief. But take solace in this assumption, *'Cause like the rolling thunder panic can roar and take control but remember that as the thunder passes by, so too the anxiety will dissipate and peace will return'*. However, while someone is treading the unyielding path, and when no human being is able to suffice the hunger for hope, just rest quietly, ask the Angels to listen. You

will be amazed at how patient the Angels are and how in time, I say in time, that which is for one's highest good will emerge. Without doubt, you will experience some form of transformation, transmutation, change.

In time God will present Himself to you, he will embrace you and you will feel loved. No words, just a peaceful presence will be enough to fill your soul and you will concede to the notion that you are loved, you are as a child of God. Unseen, unheard, Angels will constantly surround you and protect you.

Just let yourself, *'Be'*.

Whether young or old, all things come to those who wait. But, answers can't be received if you don't ask for that which you need. *'Ask and you shall receive, seek and you shall find'*.

The invitation is readily available to everyone. There are no distinctions between us; rather it is we who give society the liberty to assign labels upon us.

'Aye, right', Katie Sue often said after she briefly struggled with the loss of her faith.

Katie Sue lost her confidence and trust in people after an awful ordeal in which she was falsely accused for that which she hadn't been involved in and almost had a nervous breakdown while she waited to be vindicated. But, God was forever present. Katie Sue, fell victim when she gave what she could to help one she thought was a friend. During this period Katie Sue felt there was on-one to whom she could speak. *'It was difficult to speak to people about that which I couldn't get my head around myself. Family, doctors, priests and friends, tried to affirm me in that all would be fine. But I just felt so violated and lost'*, she said.

After a month, Katie Sue had collected at least a hundred little white feathers. *'Every morning as if timed to do so, I went out to the garden and without searching, there they were . . . feathers, so fine, so pure. You might think this crazy. But I got so much affirmation every time I found a little feather that I repeated the daily exercise for what seemed months.*

Have you any idea how powerful it was, as for every feather I found, I believed the Angels were with me and I knew all would be well' she continued.

For some people it is not easy to understand the significance of the joy experienced when a person finds something as simple as a feather. When a feather falls upon one's path, (especially for those who believe that a symbol such as a feather is representative of an Angel), it is not a normal practice to pause and to consider if there is anything untoward happening.

The immediate reaction is to believe that the Angels are even more present as in the case of Katie Sue's experience at a time when she struggled with the question, *'Turn to whom?'*

In this person's case, solace was found in her profound belief in the Angels and the label in the word of Jesus, which constantly flashed in front of her during her time of struggle as she freely said: *'If it hadn't been for my faith, I don't know what would have happened. Even when in the lowest place I called out,* **'Jesus, help me'.**

And you know what, there were times when I thought there was no God, but, for some reason, I kept calling and in time my pleading aspiration was answered. I realised that God had not gone away, he was with me all the time.'

Those wearing professional labels such as counsellors, doctors, nurses and more, offer great support and help when required. As exhibited through Katie Sue's story, vulnerability has the potential to destroy and when there is anything that gives someone a sense of hope, such must be embraced. Such must be considered to be a worthy component within the search for ultimate wholeness of self. Alongside alternative and complementary therapy, medical support and spiritual sustenance, it is good to value the celebration of self, of life and living.

Yes, there are labels attached to each of us within the world. Appearance and/or culture, class or creed are all too often used to pigeon-hole people into various boxes in society, where other people are permitted to label one another.

Yes!

Sometimes it's quite an arduous request but the secret is to reserve judgement upon others and to respect one another.

It is so easy to label someone but it is not so easy to remove that which is set upon another. As in the case of Katie Sue, she suffered with the fear of what she allowed herself to believe other people thought of her. She worried and allowed other people to henpeck her. Sometimes, we allow ourselves to be drawn into a place where we can't find answers. Other people are permitted to drive. But in time, family and friends encouraged her to surrender her worries and her fears to God and the Angels and to claim back that which was legitimately hers, her life!

Her closest friend knowing how important the Angels were to her asked her to consider if the Angels could direct her or what might they suggest—her response being, *'The Angels would ask—Whose life is it anyway?'*

A challenge is to unlearn so as to learn and to recognise the beauty of every individual: quite frequently the exterior provokes an almost expected response. Yet, there is an invitation to see what lies behind the outer surface. In life and living everyone is provoked and teased by various factors which determine how we evolve. The world of today has so much to offer. The greatest challenge is to own the choices one makes. To *'be'* real to oneself is paramount. If a religious or a professional does not believe in the service they dare to provide, then how can they dare to serve those in their care?

This practice is also applied when we wish to unveil that which lies behind the face of a person, a building, a place or even a fashion statement. Indeed, believe it or not, there is a wealth to be found within everybody, everything, every place that we come across, more precious than any words can describe!

From time to time masks hide the pain and the hurt that lies within. But reality is that we are. There is no-one destined to be anything other than self. So *'Turn to whom?'* is transparent when fear and anxiety are dissipated.

Believe and receive.

Receive and reveal.

Reveal and be true!

Responsibility is thine.

It's yours, it's mine!

Angels are yours, Angels are mine!

Angels honour God and serve to bring that which is for one's highest good but unlike the gardener they are inhibited to act without an invitation to do so. We have the responsibility to seek the help we need to attain ultimate wellbeing.

 *Ultimate wellbeing*

The main three aspects of self to be nourished so that ultimate wellbeing may be realised are the body, soul and mind. As the body houses the cogs, the mechanisms which operate the working parts of self, it is important that due care is embraced. The mind houses the power of thought, feelings and emotions and the soul houses the spiritual and sacrosanct aspects of self. There is a wealth of tools and therapies available to all; with prayerful discernment and consideration, choice is on offer.

Various therapies which are widely available within contemporary society offer so much. When performed within the basis of pure intention, no-one should be afraid.

If a therapy is founded in pure spirit, no harm can penetrate either the therapist or the recipient of the treatment.

'As a Reiki Master, I used to perform Reiki, but as time has passed I have found that rather than opening up to the universe I invoke the power of the Angels, the Holy Spirit

*and/or the Ascended Masters. This practice makes me feel
safe and so the person I share with is safely protected, cleared
and finally grounded.'* Therapies alone or together with
acupuncture, reflexology, yoga, energy healing, Reiki,
herbal medicine and beauty treatments all serve the
wellbeing of the body. When such therapies are being
carried out, there is also the possibility that such will
stretch to serve other weak areas of self.

In relation to the healing of the mind, there are many
practices available which will enhance and empower those
in need. Counsellors and psychotherapists work constantly
to help those who struggle to believe in themselves,
those who blindly deny themselves of the best life has
to offer. Many of the therapies mentioned in relation to
wellbeing of the body help the balancing of the soul and
the mind. Where there is or has been addiction, violence
and/or discord there are always people on hand who do
understand.

There is always help available.

A mental health patient in a hospital once said *'Nobody
understands. Nobody! Some days I just don't want to get up. I
just roll into a ball and lie in my room. Can you even begin
to imagine how lost I feel?'*

*I don't even want to go out. I don't want to meet people
or speak to anyone. I don't think anybody understands what
I am going through. I don't blame them, 'cause I don't know
myself. There are days I think I would be better dead, it's an
everyday struggle and I try but I just can't get better. I want to
lash out at times when people tell me to pull myself together.
Inside my head, I can feel the anger swelling so much it's as
if there is something eating me; when I am really in a bad*

place I can't hear, see and sometimes it's as if all my senses are lost. I just can't explain what it's like. Yet, when I am in a good space, I love my friends to be with me, to help me and to encourage me to do things. It's like a death sentence.

But believe this or not, I call on God and the Angels even when things aren't so good!'

This woman felt so lost. She told me that reading and learning about the Angels has been a great help with her everyday struggle to survive. When she is up, she is up. But when she is down, she is down. There rarely is any in-between.

It is so humbling and affirmative to realise the deep faith many people own. Whether it is to say a prayer, sit in silence, gather feathers, hear a whisper of affirmation, hear your name being called aloud or more, it is important to believe that God is sending a message of hope and of love.

As in this woman's case, the Angels are a powerful spiritual support and energy which is always there.

When a person is in such a place, how can we reach them? Without the help of professionals and associated trained individuals the journey is often cocooned in darkness. The very best the bystander can possibly do is to pray and to send Angels in abundance to support both the person in need and those who endeavour to help.

Angels serve to bridge the gap between Heaven and Earth. Encourage the person to embrace the light of abundance. Frequently, the soul which is the core of our being is neglected. In contemporary society people believe that there is no real leadership and somehow the shepherds have either lost their way or have lost sheep along the way.

Nourishment of the soul is a responsibility of self but there is a need for leadership in relation to spirituality. Peace, joy and happiness are a reflection of the beauty and the life of the soul.

There are many tools and implements which can help the development of the soul. The power of prayer whether such is quiet meditation, contemplation or a mix such as Lexio Divini, can all help when trying to feed the soul. Intercessory prayers, rosaries and novenas, too, can play a powerful part in helping the spirit to grow. Participating in the Eucharist is *'the'* most powerful of all, yet, unfortunately in today's society many people choose to take no notice of this gift of the Body and Blood of Christ.

The Scriptures offer us a wealth of text full of stories reflective of evolution, of humanity and faith. The Old Testament is difficult to understand or interpret, yet, the writings draw scenes reflective of society today.

The *'fight and the flight'*, the struggle for power, for glory of a human kind and the greatest story ever to be told is rooted in the words of the prophets of old. Alongside the stories of *'fight and flight'* there are powerful words of love and hope as in the Psalms and the Song of Songs. The time line of the Old Testament is powerfully captured and helps to enkindle the writings encased in the book of the New Testament. In the writings of the latter, the story is full of faith, hope and invitation to love God, He who has an unconditional love for each and every human being. There is a sense of renewal and light. Even the language is easier to read and understand.

There are also numerous spiritual books to help with the nourishment of the soul. Priests and religious serve to provide for the flock. The food of the spirit, *'the Eucharist'* followed closely with the practice of spiritual reading, personal prayer, prayer groups and reaching out to the best of one's ability to the poor, the downtrodden and those in need of support of various kinds.

Just as the approach to wholeness of well-being has become a thorny and sceptical phenomenon for some; so too the concept that an unseen, unheard spiritual being can have such a positive effect upon life and living is challenging. For some people, such is a palpable concept and for others such is embraced as an exciting and somewhat romantic theory to be considered.

It is not enough to prescribe the best for the body and ignore the needs of the mind and the soul and vice versa. Consequently, the invitation is to distinguish between what you believe you're worthy of, and not on that which someone else proposes. Embrace the life you own, live your life and enjoy the span of time allocated to that which you have received. We are encouraged to be aware to the whispers of openness inviting us just to *'be'*.

Whispers to Openness

One good act, a heartfelt act of kindness is worth more than anyone will ever know; no cost can be attached to such a gift! Frequently, we receive messages but may not be aware that such is happening. When we believe and become aware of the Angels and what they can do, we permit our hearts and mind to embrace such a gift.

Angels' whispers of openness invite us to live in a place of peace and tranquillity. In a place where the past is no longer in control, blocks and debris holding hurts, pain, anger and isolation begin to break. Jenny came along for a healing and as she settled down she confidently stated *'You know what, I don't know what I am doing here, I don't need healing.'*

I didn't respond and as she lay down she very quickly grew very serene. As the gentle music accompanied the words of the Angels, I could see her forehead lose its lines. As I invoked the healing power of the Angels her face became so relaxed, so fresh that she looked so angelic. When it was time to awake, her response was slow. As

Jenny opened her eyes, she looked up and smiled. Slowly she began to come back to reality. As she drank water she continued to smile. Patiently, I waited and then she spluttered out excitedly, *'I have to say, that was incredible. I could feel my heart get really sore and then when it eased, I felt so free, so light. I could hear the Angels whisper, asking me to open my heart, to forgive myself and learn to love myself. I didn't think I needed any healing, I just wanted to experience a renewal of cellular energy.'* This person became aware of the whisper to open her heart so as to '*be*' liberated.

Smiling again she began to tell of hurt and pain that she believed she had dealt with but which now she realised such was lurking deep within. Angel energy healing is of God, the one whom they serve. In turn these Angelic beings serve all who call for help and support and occasionally people are chosen to serve one another based on the profound belief that God is the ultimate healer.

Inner harmony develops when bounded in the truth that love is unconditional and forgiveness of self and others gives way to personal liberty. Ironically, one of the greatest sacred gifts of the Catholic tradition is that of Reconciliation. In this practice one is given the opportunity to humbly repent and seek forgiveness and atone by holding the intention to not sin again. Such is based in humility and profound belief that when one repents the soul is refreshed and cleansed.

In some respects such a practice is akin to that of spiritual counselling where a story is shared in confidence with the added gift of mercy.

When we open our hearts and our minds, we become aware of the needs of ourselves and that of others. Intuitively connected with the Angels our level of awareness heightens and messages from the highest spiritual sphere are meaningful and right.

Cassie tells this story. *'One night before a Saint Padre Pio Mass, there was a man sitting at the back of the chapel, with his head cupped in his hands. It was obvious by the alcoholic stench that he was drunk. Some people asked to have him removed from the chapel but I called out to him. I brought the man back into the chapel and sat him at the rear of the church. He said to me with a tear falling, "I have nowhere to go. I was going to the river and then noticed the chapel was opened, so I came in." After Mass was over, a parishioner took him back to his own home. A few weeks later a member of his family informed me that he had stopped drinking and was getting better. Now about five years on, he is still sober both in body and mind; he attends daily Mass and has found a sense of profound peace.'*

As in the words of Dorothy Day, take time to consider when one meets or greets someone. In actual fact, as portrayed in the film *'You may be entertaining Angels'*, we come across God in His entirety of spirit in encounters, words and deeds to those whom we meet. Scriptural references are recorded in: Hebrews 1:1-3; Psalms 118:6-7; Romans 12:13 and Matthew 25:38.

Recently, at an *Angel Awareness Day*, I chose to talk about Dorothy Day. This woman is a modern day example of selflessness and unconditional love, an Angel in disguise!

Dorothy Day was born in New York in 1897 and died in 1980. As a young girl, Dorothy Day lived quite an unsavoury, sometimes rather seedy life style, living in common law relationships, chose to have an abortion (which tortured her mind) and consistently rebelled against authority. She pursued a career in journalism and was a social activist and was the co-founder of the Catholic Worker Movement.

In 1927 she became a Roman Catholic and now with a child, and supported by a group of friends, she devoted her life to the service of others. Together, they published a newspaper, the income of which was used to feed the hungry and house the homeless. Her life story is powerful; her daily human struggle for self and the social plight of fellow human beings brought her face to face with God, Church and State. She is a model pro-life lay witness and intercessor. She was chosen as the 20th century's most outstanding lay Catholic. *"If I have achieved anything in my life,"* she once remarked, *"it is because I have not been embarrassed to talk about God."*

At the end of the morning session of the *Angel Awareness Day*, among a number of individuals who talked with me, there was an American lady accompanied by her brother who approached me.

As she greeted me, she said, *'My brother and I are from New York. We just happened to see an advertisement about this 'Getting to know the Archangels Day' and as we are stopping close by, we decided to come along. I frequently work in the Bronx and can relate very much to what has been shared today.*

Nothing just happens; there is a reason for everything. So, just thought you should be aware, that my brother works tirelessly for the cause of the beatification of Dorothy Day, considered by Church and society to be a modern day candidate for sainthood. I couldn't believe it when you started to talk about someone from New York, never mind Dorothy Day. Can you imagine how my brother reacted when you chose to talk about Dorothy Day and entertaining Angels?'

It was only the previous night while preparing for the day's talk that the notion to mention Dorothy Day entered my head. I am sure you can imagine how, initially, I was amazed. But then I thought: God had sent His ministering agents, my spiritual guides, to nudge me to deliver a message to these persons and more.

The lady then went on to tell me this story: *'A young woman was out with friends for a night and on returning home, which was then the early hours of the morning, she decided to take a near cut to her home. As she made her way up a dimly lit alley way, she became aware that there was a male figure standing by the wall beyond her.*

After considering turning back, she decided she might draw more attention, so she nervously continued to make her way towards the man. Before she approached him, she prayed that God would send an Angel to protect her. As she passed him by she felt a great sense of peace and she made her way safely home.

However, the next morning, it was announced on a local radio that a woman had been attacked and killed at that very alley way she had walked through earlier that morning. The woman was murdered at that very spot where she had encountered the scary character. It was said that a man had been charged with the rape and the murder of a lone female victim.

On hearing this story, she made her way to the precinct and explained her experience and asked to see the man under arrest. *After a number of pleas, the police permitted her to be accompanied to meet the man.*

Looking into his dismal eyes, she asked: "Why did you not attack me? I passed you by and you didn't attempt to attack me."

He responded by saying, "You gotta be joking lady. With the big hunk beside you, I didn't dare." At this instant she realised that her belief that God had protected her was affirmed. God had indeed sent His Angel to protect her from harm.' So never underestimate the power of the Angels, as in the latter story, the presence of an Angel was a protective presence in a time of potential danger. There is no doubt that God really heard and responded to that woman's call for help.

As in the case of the young woman and her experience of Angelic assistance, another lady shared the following story of how that which was lost was found and was the catalyst in her opening herself up to embracing a deeper faith.:

'My daughter and myself were walking through the park. It was coming up near midnight. The moon was really bright and resembled a rugby ball; it was an oval shape.

It was very peaceful.

It was so peaceful it was almost eerie.

We both noticed the sudden change in the shape of the moon. Suddenly, the enlarged ball grew almost white and looked as if it were descending. Nervously, we clung to each other as we watched the moon spit out particles of glistening droplets around us. As each little droplet fell by us we tried to catch them but it was impossible. The bright sky grew dim before a burst of sparkling white light broke through the flawless frosty sky. The beam of white light lit up the path.

The light shone like a gigantic torch unto a body lying by an overhanging sycamore tree.

We held on even tighter to each other and tiptoed towards the body covered in a blanket of cardboard. It took us quite some time to pluck up the courage to approach the crouched up body.

With Anna's hands clutching me, I reached down and after a second glance noticed that the sleeping individual looked familiar. Jumping back, I tramped on Anna's toes and she reacted by gasping out so loud that the figure began to stir.

Again, I moved towards the body, reached forward and beckoned the unshaven man to sit up. Tears began to fall down my cheeks.

At that minute, I realised, that the man in the cardboard dwelling was my estranged brother, Noel, who had been missing for ever.

He didn't know me at first.

Anna had never met him but had often heard the story of how her uncle Noel had disappeared and was never found.

I hugged him but he was still distant and unsure. He was so stiff, he was like a board. The moon grew exceedingly bright as I reached forward to claim that which was lost and now was found. For years and years, we prayed that one day Noel would be found alive.

There is little doubt that both of our parents died with broken hearts but somewhere in the greater picture, there was the notion that they worked from that place of grace to allow Noel and his estranged family to be reunited.

Often, we wished that our parents had seen Noel before their passing but we realise and accept it was not to be.

Finally, our prayers were answered.

It was amazing.

It was and still is hard to believe but it did happen, Noel is living with us now. Anna and I often think if this had occurred while either of us were alone, the outcome may have been very different. For one, who would dare to believe that such could happen?

I still have goose bumps when I recall that night! I could so easily have walked away. It was just meant to be . . . .

There was a time when it seemed all hope had faded but it goes to show you, there is a God.' When we are confronted with a challenge, we have the ability to be courageous in attempting to help where possible. When any act of humanity is carried out in pure intention, you can be sure the Angels are at work; quite often we are the vessels where the help for another is stored.

And when the need arises, the Angels, through us, serve those in need of help and support. We all trod the same path of life and living, but in our own footsteps and not those of others. Occasionally we may be unaware that our footsteps stop for a moment; God carries us through the maze of uncertainty, illness, loneliness, worry or fear; it's His footsteps that are visible, not yours, not mine!

Jenna worked in the outbacks of Chile. When she was there she encountered an experience that changed her life as she has revealed. *'A priest friend, Father Phelim, travelled many miles every week on an old black bicycle, you know, one of those heavy built bikes of the forties! (laughing)*

One week, a young tribesman asked to accompany him to the unit where medical care was performed. As I was a doctor, I was invited to go, too. But, with only one bicycle, it was agreed that we would all travel by foot. The journey by foot was tough and took just under seven hours. When we arrived we were ushered into a make shift holding. It had all the hall marks of the buildings depicted in the American twentieth century film 'The Inn of the Sixth Happiness' starring Ingrid Bergman, based on the true story of Gladys Aylward, who despite her lack of education and rejection, became a missionary in China.

It was eerie, I could almost feel the presence of Gladys Aylward and felt as if I were chosen to walk in her steps as a missionary serving those in need.

The holding was sparsely furnished. There were two hammocks alongside one wall; a shelved wall which served as a larder and a dispensary. In the middle of the dust covered floor there was a table on which a lantern was lit. With only two chairs if one could describe them as such, most of us gathered together sat on old sacks on the ground. Being generally quite squeamish, I constantly watched as mites and flies dipped in and out of the utensils sitting on the table.

Night was closing in and to quell my obvious edginess it was suggested that we pray. In the dimly lit room, again, I could feel this other presence. As we prayed I could hear a voice whisper 'This is your time', over and over in mantra form.

I could feel myself fighting sleep. The peace and tranquillity were indescribable. There was a sweet smell not unlike incense but there was nothing obvious. Father Phelim wore a stole as he blessed each of us gathered together.

As the final prayer was said our travel companion stood up. He stood tall and silent. We watched but no-one moved. Then he produced a knife. Turning the knife towards himself he cried out in anger and swung towards me. I could feel the life within me drain. Just as the knife came towards me one of the other volunteers grabbed him from behind and knocked the knife to the ground. It was a strange happening. It was absurd to say the least. Yet, I often believe that the spiritual presence of Gladys Aylward was the Angel of protection sent to save me from harm. Sometimes, I pinch myself when I tell this story but the presence of an Angel is forever with me.'

Jenna's story had a powerful impact upon those whom she worked with in Chile and later in Africa. The effect of her inner peace transcends freely through her work as a missionary. The effects of her presence are embraced with love by those in her care and in her humanness she understands the need for liberation.

You know what it's like when you feel hard done by or you're down in the dumps, and out of the blue something extraordinary happens, whether it is something great or small, such can quickly jerk you back into reality. Even if only for an instant, the tinted glasses fall down and all becomes clear, such is powerfully enlightening and helps to distinguish between the affect and the effect of external influence.

 *Affect or Effect?*

Do other people dictate how you live, where you live, who or what you live for? Excuses may be made for people of past generations who were relatively innocent, in the sense that they quite willingly supposed those in authority to be right, that they followed their direction without occasion of public opposition.

Do you allow the influence of others to affect you? Are you persuaded to *'yes'* rather than say *'no'*? Can you allow yourself to *'be'*? Can you believe and trust yourself to make an appropriate decision? In trusting yourself such reflects the profound faith of God within you.

When one becomes *'Grace filled'*, one no longer seeks the biggest and the best but becomes awakened to the frequent Angelic whispers that nudge us to perceive the depth of love and hope that fills the littlest of words, thoughts and deeds.

It's the littlest of things that transform us!

'One day when my mum wasn't feeling too good, a woman whom she hadn't seen for quite a while arrived.

114

No warning!

No phone call, nothing!

Well, it was as if my mum had won the lotto. The visit of that woman reignited a light that was growing dim. The stories and the yarns were so full of life. The radiant glow shone over my mum for a considerable length of time, as she and her friend revisited the memories that meant so much. As they talked their journey into the past took flight. There was an excitement as they recalled people whom they worked with at the 'Mill' and the long walks to get to the dances.'

In the space of an hour a soul was given a sense of renewed energy.

It's absolutely amazing how we very seldom realise the effect a visit can have on a person living alone, someone housebound as a result of illness, a person suffering from anxiety, depression or any affliction which excludes them from the outside world.

Yes!

Little things mean so much!

Have you any idea what it is like to be starved of company? When we are blessed with relatively good health we can never be fully aware of what it is like for someone who is confined to their home. Maybe, just maybe, we frequently take so much for granted.

We can't help that.

Afterall, in our basic humanness when things are going well, we don't consider what it would be like if it were otherwise!

However, one of the nicest things to experience is simply to know that you have been missed, that you matter. Whether it's because your routine is to go to town every day, or go the Chapel everyday or go to a particular group weekly and for whatever reason you have had to opt out for a time, there's just something lovely when you are told that you're missed.

Such was the case of how Angels looked out for Bill and who in time brought him a sense of great peace. Living in a housing executive flat, Bill estranged from his wife and family had become a very angry man.

The world owed him!

Or so he believed.

He couldn't perceive that he owed anything to anybody. He genuinely couldn't believe that he was to blame in any way for the breakup of the family. *I worked hard. I worked all the hours God sent. The wife, she wanted for nothing, she got everything she wanted. Around the house I tirelessly worked to keep up appearances. It was constant: need this, need that; new this, new that. I was so fed-up I would get really angry. I got the boys through college. I built up a great home. Over the years I saved and managed to get a better car, and then a work van. I did this, I did that. But nothing was ever good enough. My family wanted for nothing. Then after thirty years everything fell apart. I was thrown out; I went back and eventually I was told point blankly that I wasn't wanted. I wasn't needed and I wasn't loved. After this, I took to the drink; I ran to dances, I felt like a young man again but couldn't find peace. Then one day, I went along to a Divine Mercy talk, and found many people there in search of peace. I looked at the picture of the Divine Mercy and the coloured rays of light in the picture seemed to be alive. It was as if the God's healing rays of light were pouring into me burning the inner bitterness I felt.*

Angels were before me and around me. I felt their presence. Since that venture I have never had to battle with anger. I have reconciled with family and I now live a very peaceful and serene life. Sometimes, I pinch myself to remind myself of what life was and now what life is for me!'

Angelic deliverance affects us all when we allow the Angels to work, to act and to help. Angel messages frequently come to us. With an open heart and an open mind Angelic presence is felt. So, be aware, accept and acknowledge the existence of God's gift.

Angels, your heavenly guides and protectors, will never try to direct or influence anyone's thoughts, words or deeds. They patiently await the call of those who believe they can help. God in his loving kindness has given everyone the great gift of '*free will*'. Therefore, with the utmost respect Angels wait to serve. Can you imagine what it's like for them to see the man-made destruction taking place in the world; the unrest and wars against society, church and more?

Destruction in modern society is prevalent within bullying which unfortunately occurs all too often in the workplace, in the home, in the various sectors that steer society. The vulnerable individuals who are on the receiving end are quite powerless and don't know how to react or deal with the incurring fear. Cyber bullying has become a destructive means of harassment. The silent fear and tear of the vulnerable young person, adult and victim of any maltreatment is reflective of that which is of evil. Sometimes, Angels weep while they wait and it is their tears that fall amidst the showers. Therefore, be not afraid, when confronted with such negativity, just call upon the Angels who wish to serve.

When the Angels are invited to help, it is difficult to describe the joy they experience. Every time they deliver a message from God, they dance and sing. What a person does with the response to their quest is their own responsibility as Angels can't bring anything more at that precise moment. War and peace of varying design and natures are the extremities everyone experiences at some time. But it's good to know there is always help at hand.

Life and living are influenced as a result of centuries of discord, conflict and revolutions in which people fought for what was perceived to be the ideals rather than considering the constants in place. The nineteen sixties saw great changes within society, people embraced a period of '*free love*'. As '*the Beatles*' emerged as Pop idols sharing songs affirming us '*That all we need is love, love, love*'. Wouldn't it be great if that was all anyone needed to exist?

Reality is rather more complex.

Alongside such changes, the Church began to seek change. In an attempt to transform itself, Vatican II opened debate onto the public domain. This was a shift in the Church's endeavours to bring about a greater balance between Church and laity. Strangely enough such gave way to a period of discord and discontentment.

Why?

First of all, it is important to note that in endeavouring to please, there is always the possibility that such efforts will initially be rejected. Change of attitudes and understanding provoke people to look for the *'catch'*, the underlying question: *'What's in it for you?'*

Consequently, it is difficult to notice the attempts being made by others to create a more transparent world, full of love, hope and faith in one another. Trust must be overcome to move forward with a people invited to play a greater role in that which was an established entity.

As a society, we are no longer afraid to argue our point of view. To a greater rather than lesser degree, we are not afraid of authority at any level. The profound respect our ancestors had for Church and society have weakened significantly, to the extent that some people genuinely don't see the need to conform. Some people refuse to conform and indeed some people abuse such issues to meet their own beliefs/agendas.

In contemporary society and contemporary Church, we no longer suffer scruples which were a big problem for generations of the past. In many respects it is good that such attitudes have been squelched and that a more open agenda has been put forward, where we are encouraged to search, to learn, to listen and to embrace the real loving God.

As a greater awareness and shift of consciousness seeks attention we begin to realise there is an abundance of help and support readily available for all. God's love is readily available.

We are encouraged to envisage God not as a fearful ogre, a gruesome giant, but rather that of the BFG, the Big Friendly Giant, with a heart so big that there is room for everyone.

Abundance

Abundance in plenty is there for those who seek.
Think abundance and it's yours. When negative thoughts are permitted to develop, pessimism overrides positive thinking.

However, when the Angels refer to abundance, what do you consider they are talking about? They refer to the great gifts which are there despite being unseen and/or indescribable. In a material world the understanding of abundance is reflective of plenty in relation to wealth, health and social standing and more. Unfortunately, there will be those who don't aspire to such need. Yet, from a spiritual stance they may be actually better-off in having spiritual abundance over material wealth.

We are encouraged to seek the best for self and those around us. It is a human trait to either experience *'fight or flight'*. In so doing, quite often, people do not pause to think of what is happening. When one is wealthier than another, is it difficult to perceive what life is like for those less fortunate? Ironically, the less well-off in monetary terms may be wealthier than one could ever begin to imagine, as they have an abundance of spiritual wealth.

Yet, the Angels, serve to support and help everyone who calls upon them with pure intention. Angels are first and foremost messengers of God. The amount of help and guidance available to all is plentiful; there is enough to serve everyone. God does not make a difference between you, me, us. God wishes only to make life and living as rich as it can ever be; that is, rich in body, soul and mind.

Within the ongoing journey, Angels watch and wait as we endeavour to survive in the world God designed for us to enjoy. Love in abundance is the great gift from which you were formed. God's love is so powerful that from a human point of view, for some people, such can prove to be a very difficult concept to understand and appreciate.

Believe in abundance and abundance shall be yours! Let abundance of spirit *'be'* yours!

During the days that roll out through the journey of life and living, diversions and road blocks within the body, soul and mind may create upheaval and discord, but Angels are ready to respond when called upon. The balance of body, soul and mind are paramount and we have a responsibility to claim the best.

Help in abundance is at hand.

Do you believe that?

In an attempt to understand the expectations of family, friends and more, the Angels have to take time out occasionally to realise what it is that you need to fulfil your life and living. Gentle patience and peacefulness gives way to great gifts. While Angels can't promise you wealth, health or happiness, what they can promise is they will act swiftly and lovingly to do what they can to make life better. Angels will only serve that which is for one's highest good.

Sometimes, people say, *'If the Angels can do such great things, why can't they give us the lotto numbers?'*

Whoo!

Angels may see this as a humorous jibe. But such can't alter the directives they receive as they take on the role as spiritual mentors and/or guides. Angels rank in command and are ordered by Archangels who are closest to God. Now, can you begin to imagine what it would be like if God gave the Angels permission to give such information? The abundance on offer from the highest sphere is based solely on the good that will enhance life and living, that which will enhance one's ultimate wellbeing.

What is abundance?

Abundance refers to that of plenty.

Abundance fundamentally points to that of a large or great quantity.

There are extremes to both sides of the meaning of abundance.

On the one hand, there is the overloading, too much, overwhelming amounts which have the potential of being abused. While, on the other hand, there is the scarcity, where there is poverty or an insufficiency which can give way to anxiety, worry, stress and much more.

A great gift is to have the faith to believe in having enough; having an efficient amount to live and survive will envelop you in peace. Such will satisfy you and secure you in your life and living.

We only have to look at the media and magazines to consider how relatively well-off we really are!

'Speak for yourself', you may suggest—that's okay. But in reality the poverty of the Third World is so great that we can't even begin to imagine their needs. In the midst of all the drama that such poverty reveals there are many Earth Angels who constantly volunteer to help those in need. An abundance of love, hope and faith are the essential ingredients needed in living a truly meaningful life. Everyone can claim abundance by seeking the help and support they need.

When an open heart and an open mind are embraced, connection with the Angels may become more transparent. Relationships with the Angels will develop easily when one is peaceful.

Angels and Relationships

Another area to be considered is that of relationships. Angels can assist if only we would permit them to do so. Angels and relationships do have credence in relation to helping to ease the pain of feeling let down, no longer loved and/or ostracised, pushed aside.

The greatest secret within the breakdown of marriage and/or relationships is that of each person involved having the humility to listen, to try to understand and forgive.

Aye right!

A range of excuses usually emerge without little thought e.g. *'It was his/her fault: if he/she hadn't gone to such and such this wouldn't have happened: he/she doesn't love me anymore: he/she is a bully: he/she is a flirt and I can't cope with that: if he/she loved me, he/she couldn't have put someone else before me/us'.*

On the surface some of these examples may seem rather petty but to someone who is vulnerable, insecure in themselves such can impact upon them more than anyone can comprehend. It may be hard to believe that there are many people who carry secrets imprisoned in their hearts and that in the past devoid of the contemporary form of self help available, many secrets were taken to the grave. No matter how close one maybe with another the hidden pressure of such may weigh more heavily than ever could be imagined.

A young woman who was subjected to an ordeal which heavily weighed upon her, said: *'When I was twelve years old, a man who called regularly to our home scared me so much. My parents were out but we as a family were all in the living room. The stench of alcohol still lingers in my nostrils when I think of this man. Despite the others in the room, he pushed me down into the sofa. Then he held me down. I'll never forget the strength of his grip on my arms.*

Even though I was squealing, it was as if everyone else thought it was funny. As he leant over me he repeatedly said, "Give us a kiss, give us a kiss . . . ." a phrase which has continued to haunt me every time I think of this encounter. To adults of that era I was told, 'It was only a bit of fun' but to this day I live with the deep anger, resentment and abuse associated with this act. Children don't understand that which adults perceive to be funny, within a child's mind the fear is so terrible that it is like a cancer gnawing away within'.

The strange thing about this story is that despite the fear the then-child experienced, the parents were willing to play this down and permit the other person to continue to visit. This was not the case in another story shared with me.

Gen, a mature woman allowed herself to confront a man who had abused her as a child. *'I told my parents and* my granny that the man who called every week often pulled me to sit on his knee. One night, I tried to hide when I knew he was coming. I got so sick. I was shaking inside just as I feel now that I recall what happened. When he came in, he asked where I was . . . . for some it may seem funny but I was terrified when I heard him coming upstairs. I hid under the bed. My granny who lived with us told him to get down stairs and as she did I came out from under the bed. I was so scared that I had wet myself. Granny spoke to me, washed me and took me by the hand downstairs.

I was trembling.

I felt sick.

Then my granny asked the man to take a good look at the state I was in. I can remember how cross she was as she said, "Get out of this house and don't come back. You're not welcome and don't ever tease or annoy my grand-daughter ever again." Without any exchange of words, he left the house and never visited again, not even after my granny died.

She was my Angel.

I was listened to. I wasn't just a child. I mattered. My fear was destroying me. She always told me to pray for that man. Initially, I couldn't understand why. It was as if he were the victim. Then in time I began to realise that in praying for him, peace was allowed to flourish.'

Sometimes, it seems that all too often people throw the towel in too quickly. This is not to say that all situations can be repaired; but that there is a need to try to mend the brokenness between each other and to achieve an amicable outcome. Ultimately, this is a basic Christian act that can permit an understanding, a sense of reconciliation and forgiveness, yielding to either renewal or an agreed separation.

It is a reasonable assumption to perceive the influence of others, whether it is spouse, family members, friends or school/work mates. Inevitably, such influence decision-making, beliefs and indeed Christian practice.

Faith is fundamentally a personal attribute which may have been inherited as a result of family or culture; we may have been born into a particular faith, tradition or culture.

The challenge is to hold onto the great power which accompanies such a characteristic founded in the love, hope and faith based in God's unconditional love and mercy.

God's love is unconditional and the messengers who serve to illumine the path to help us become aware that we deserve the best life can give are Angels. From time to time, it may seem difficult to believe that you, me, we are worthy of help and support. As Angels wait, listen and desire to work to help all in need.

Within the heavenly realm there are hosts of Angels readily available to respond to one's call. They know when you are in need but they do not have the permission to act or intervene without an invitation to do so. We need to be aware of how difficult it is for Angels to stand by and to wait when they are aware of your pain, your hurt, your anger or when you are struggling with ill health, abuse, addiction, marital breakdowns, loneliness, anxiety, depression and/or loss.

Angels watch from the periphery, the outside, as they wait close by. When we open to the notion that Angels, the messengers of God, exist and that they can help and act on our behalf, then the awareness will lead to acceptance and eventual acknowledgement of the power of the Angels. If you can realise the development from consciousness to acceptance, you will inevitably embrace the spiritual growth and the slow but constant transformation of self.

Albeit a slow and persistent journey, you accept and begin to recognize the value of what the Angels can do for you. When the step to acceptance is taken, it is then you can realise that there is so much more they can do for you than you may ever have imagined. Support and guidance is not dependant on status, class or creed.

No!

Help is readily available to all who call. They swiftly take your requests and concerns to God. They act as quickly as they can. Sometimes they will respond so fast, you'll not know what's happening. We may have to wait on a response; we can't dictate the pace. But they will prompt God when you feel you're being ignored. Just remember, all prayers are answered, maybe not in the way we want but in a way that what is for our highest good will be granted.

Acceptance to the existence, the power and the healing transmuted through the Angels, gives way to liberation from the old school of thought, thought patterns of past generations. The healing power of the Angels has become an exciting phenomenon embraced by people of all faith traditions. The beautiful feeling of a Heavenly presence and belief that Angels do exist, has for many, provided a greater sense of belonging. Awareness and acceptance of

God's love for each of us, is revealed in His crucifixion and death.

God has given each of us an Angel and in some cases many people believe they have a number of Angels to support them, to help and to accompany them along the path of life and living, the journey of life.

We are invited to believe, embrace and unlearn, so as to learn how to seek the best life has to offer. Angels are of God. Angels are God's link with this world. Angels honour God as they joyfully serve humanity.

Within the profound belief that Angels serve to enhance one's life and living, it is with great joy that they celebrate when we become aware and accept the goodness that embodies our being. Appreciation is when one has fully opened to all the gifts available. When we become appreciative of the awareness and acceptance of the Angels and the relationships which develop, the invitation is to acknowledge how powerful God is! Just call.

Without faith in the Angels, it is impossible to acknowledge the existence, the healing power and the service they are intended to carry out.

When you believe and allow Angels into your life, have you any idea how much this means to them? It's their gift to God when they can serve you, me, us. They are God's gift to you. If you believe, then in turn, your life is your gift to God.

What do you do with a gift?

Do you accept such and really appreciate the same? Would you agree that it would be rude to throw a gift aside, or out of sight? Likewise, if your life is a gift from

God, then the best compliment would surely be to make the most out of it and to look after your life.

In turn, the appreciation of your life is the greatest gift you can give to God. It is in trusting you become aware and can accept and appreciate what the Angels can do for you and to be thankful for the great love God has for you.

 *Beauty*

The old cliché is, *'Beauty is in the eye of the beholder'*. Yet, how often can we see the beauty that is within those we meet, those we serve, the animals, the earth, the good, the bad and the ugly and even ourselves? We are all worthy of recognition and affirmation.

Have you ever seen the vulnerability in a distressed person's face; have you noticed how the eyes of a child change when happy or sad; have you experienced that moment when there is no apparent beauty, yet, the serenity and happiness emanated from another overwhelms you?

So, how do we wish others to see us?

The invitation is to see the beauty of others as we see it in ourselves. Do we see God within ourselves? When we say that we do, we also see God in those we encounter.

Well, do you concur with this statement? Generally, it would seem fair to agree that beauty is that which is observed by the admirer or the looker-on. Either way, beauty basically refers to all that is good, that which is attractive, lovely or exquisite. Beauty has the advantage of that which is ugly, there is no argument, but there is an amount of truth that the beauty and the beast exist within each and every one of us.

Yes!

We may not wish to admit such an assumption. But while the beauty has the gift of attraction, the ugly component of jealousy raises its head. Can you begin to imagine what it is like for Angels to witness the attack of the green-eyed monster upon the soul searching to exhibit nothing only good?

Within the action of one who is referred to as a close friend, who secretly tries to make little of you or break you down, it is so difficult to understand what is happening. Such experiences, if not dealt with appropriately, can give way to revenge, anger, and behavioural actions contrary to one's normal disposition.

Julie shared her story. *'I am a real soft touch. I always look out for the underdog. I guess I have learnt that there is such a thing as humility; and there is such a thing as stupidity. A couple of years ago I opened my door to someone in need. The loneliness of this person shone out like a lamp. There was a strange beauty in the person, vulnerability or so it seemed. Anyway, cutting a long story short, I encouraged my family to help. When the water ran dry so to speak, the person threw everything back in our faces and created great discord between us all.'*

Have you encountered a person who appears lonely and vulnerable and in your naivety lures you to the point where you do all you can to help and support them, to be rebuked and accused falsely so that they can pick up the pieces and get on with life and living?

And you, where are you?

At a guess it would seem probable that you have slipped into the dark abyss where your faith seems to have disappeared. Angels can see what is happening but can't intervene. But, when you regain a sense of hope and call upon Angels for help, they are there in full force.

Beauty, by its very nature, will inevitably encounter jealous occurrences. But again, look out for the better happenings in connection with beauty. Within the soul there is a pureness that no-one can ever steal from you. It is true that occasionally the pureness may grow dull and become slightly stained.

So!

There is nothing that can't be improved if you set your mind to make it better. There is no stain so great that such can't be eradicated or at least lessened to a degree. Angels desire to work with you to make life and living as easy as possible. When celebrations take place, allow the Angels to join in the fun. They too, like to sing and dance. When you embrace the Angels as your spiritual guides they can illumine your beauty. Through your inner beauty you will shine out among those in your company and your peaceful presence will have a ripple effect within the gathering. Never underestimate the power of the illuminated soul.

When the soul is at peace, the soul lights up all around and its energy is powerful.

Yeah! Yeah!

I know you are trying to get your head around that idea. But be assured that this does work. In a very subtle way your very presence will speak volumes in an unspoken manner; your wordless presence will vibrate throughout the room. Your smile will illumine your surroundings and the vibrancy of your spirit will reach out to others without you having to do anything.

Oh!

How happy Angels are to be around you and within your very being.

Recognise the beauty within and allow such to convince the eye of the beholder who observes the light of your soul. Angels are so honoured to work for your highest good!

Just remember: Angels are on call, twenty four seven, three six five (24-7 365).

Betrayal

Betrayal simply refers to disloyalty, infidelity, unfaithfulness and/or falseness. Frequently, Angels hear people call upon them when people feel let down by others, especially those closest to them. While Angels observe all that is happening, it is impossible for them to help if not invited to do so. Therefore, *'Do not be afraid'*, help is at hand. An answer to your quest will be received. Angels can't promise or imagine what the answer will be. But they can guarantee that that which is for one's best will emerge. Trust and surrender all the pain and the hurt of the experience over to God. Why should you, we, give the power to another who has betrayed us, to ruin life in anyway? Life is yours, life is mine, and no-one has the right to abuse that which does not belong to them.

Take a moment.

Now, gently close your eyes as you consider to rest in the Spirit of God. When you are composed and ready to take a further step, consider the following: balance the books, do a bit of soul keeping and ask yourself if there is a deficit between the good and the not so good encounters which help form you into the person you are at this moment in time. Can you begin to recognise the discrepancies and identify that which eats away at you? When you start such an exercise, frequently most people are amazed at how much good there is within the experiences and encounters to date and the positive impact such can have on life and living. Strangely enough in our basic humanness it is so easy to look for faults rather than noticing the mountain of good stored within.

That's o.kay!

There's none of us perfect: if we search for perfection, one thing is for sure, that valuable time will be wasted. Perfection can't ever be. But what we can experience is the reality of imperfection. The best we can ever try to achieve is to obtain the perfection of imperfection. By the very nature of our mortal birth we come into this earth with the indelible mark upon our soul, as a consequence of the fall of Adam & Eve in the Garden of Eden.

Such leads to the realisation that despite the small but permanent mark upon our soul, there is great joy in knowing that we are not lost; we still belong to God, and in time will return to heaven. Unceasingly, the Angels wait to help us in our tasks. Whether life is like a merry-go-round or a roller coaster, opportunities will continue to arise when the presence of an Angel will be a sufficient support in time of need.

In the silence, it is not strange to hear your name being called aloud; it is not peculiar to one person more than another; a simple feather may fall upon your path or turn up in the most unexpected place and such may be enough to confirm the presence of the Angels. Believe it or not, the encounter with someone may seem out of the ordinary at first but in time may very well reveal something very different, maybe even unveil a message from a loved one; give a reassurance that all is well. A bird, a butterfly, a bumble bee may rest by you as you either think or pray for a loved one or a special intention and such presence is recognition of the pure intention.

It is true; to some people, scepticism may create a blockage. Somewhere, somehow, for some reason there is another force at work. This does not mean that there is anything untoward happening. It simply may be that there is an internal struggle going on between the soul and the mind.

Never underestimate the power of self.

We strive to survive; we have to choose between '*fight and flight*', and as human beings we are cautious by nature and slow to surrender.

A word of warning!

Try not to allow the negative experiences such as betrayal by a loved one or one close to you, to destroy your faith, your fundamental beliefs and your trust. Rely on the truth that there are trustworthy people who desire the best for you. Call upon the Angel guides when you are in need, just call 24-7 365.

Rest in the knowledge and the love Angels can bring to you from God. With their help and support, pain can be eradicated and peace and trust can be restored. Just call . . . . Angels are not ever that far away; just by your shoulder, now that's not far, is it? Learn to forgive the one who betrays for the problem is theirs.

Pray that in time they may see the error of their ways and that in time they may become aware of the power and the healing energy of the Angels. When we rid ourselves of the pain of the past, we can begin to see through the eyes of the body, soul and mind. When we forgive ourselves, we grow in faith; we trust in hope and embrace love. When we forgive another who has abused or harmed us in any way, God sends an abundance of Angels to celebrate in the liberty of self.

Forgiveness

Now this is a challenge.

Forgiveness may be a difficult undertaking! Yet, if we really believe we can become reconciled even when we are battered and bruised, worn and torn.

There was no-one more battered and bruised or worn and torn as Jesus, who surrendered to the will of the Father. In the Lord's Prayer we are challenged to forgive and to ask for deliverance: *'And forgive us our trespasses as we forgive those who trespass against us, and lead us not into temptation but deliver us from evil.'*

In Scripture, one of the greatest themes is one of Forgiveness. Within the Old Testament many of the stories help us to understand the idea of forgiving another. We also realise the forgiveness of God. The stories of atonement in the New Testament invite us to realise how forgiveness can change one's life as a consequence of God's forgiveness.

Many years ago, Sherrie spent her life looking after her aging parents. So often she felt angry and resented other family members who had chosen to get on with their own lives. As a young teenager, Sherrie had a child to a neighbouring man who was married and with family. Her parents gave her and her child a place to live with a condition that she would care for them. It seemed a reasonable deal at the time. But as her child grew older and eventually went off to college, she realised the trap that she had been drawn into.

'My mother continually reminded who looked out for me and my son. My father rarely uttered a word. I just seemed to be weighed down with deep anger, hatred, hurt, pain . . . . the list was endless. When my father died, my mother became even more dependent on me. I felt I was going to crack up. Then one day, out of the blue a beggar came to the door.

On opening the door the unshaven and rather shabbily dressed, quite aged looking individual asked if we could give him something to eat and to drink.

I nodded.

I closed the door and went through to the kitchen to get some food and a drink for him. As I returned and opened the door I noticed that the old person was now sitting on the low wall to the front of the house. I approached him and he reached out for the food and the drink. He thanked me and blessed me over and over. As he went off, I watched the lonely figure meander down the street. Suddenly I realised that I was more fortunate that I had noticed. I could see beyond the pain and the hurt, the anger and the hatred that I had been nursing and could actually see a bigger picture.

I looked for help.

I wasn't into this modern idea that Angels could help me. Afterall, I knew I had a Guardian Angel but that was it!

I came across a woman who carried out Angel healing therapy. During one of the sessions, I had an outburst in which I cried and almost broke my heart. The meditation was based on forgiveness of self and of others. As her hands moved high above my body, I could feel healing energies penetrate my being. The debris of the past began to break and it was as if an earthquake had occurred, as if an explosion had erupted. After a number of visits a fantastic change happened.

I permitted myself to be worthy of love and deep forgiveness for myself, my parents and my next door neighbour.

The journey of my life had turned unto a smooth and less windy path. I have a peace that I could never have thought possible. I am happy. I get on well with all my family and I just dote upon my now frail beautiful mother.'

Sometimes, we just go about our daily chores and don't stop to consider what we are carrying about with us day after day. Consider some of the following—

Have you ever held a grudge?

Can you imagine the effect this has on you?

Have you ever been hurt badly?

Can you forgive that person?

Do you notice how anger and resentment sap away one's energies and one's desire to '*be*'?

Can you believe that forgiveness in really a profound act of kindness to self? Angels too show kindness when we permit them to help us!

Kindness

Kindness is an act reflective of that of an Angel. When one puts themselves into a place where they can act to help or assist a person in need, it is an extension of the spirit within.

One's connection with the Angels is then profound and so in an emergency you may very well be called upon to carry out the work of the Angels. Such an understanding is never immediately recognised; but your openness permits the Angels to work through you.

The tiniest act of kindness can penetrate the darkness. It is so important to realise that even the smallest act used to help another is more powerful than one can ever imagine. Never underestimate the power of any act of kindness. Selflessness is reflective of the kind-heartedness of a caring person who observes the needs of another and tries to enhance their situation. An act of neighbourliness, in a time of loss or illness can never be measured; such an act is from the heart.

Kitty, freely tells a story of how her mum's kindness helps her when her father died:

'Daddy suffered for a few months before he died. But, I was in denial and really believed he would get better. The morning daddy died, my mum prayed for his release.

God! I was so annoyed with her.

I didn't want him to die.

As she sat and held his hand, my daddy raised his head and smiled as he stared towards the altar by the window. On the table, there was a statue of the Virgin Mary, a crucifix and two candlesticks with two blessed candles burning. As he lifted his head, he smiled first at my mum, around each of us in the room and settled as he gazed at the altar. Instantly my mum began to pray the 'Hail Mary' and as she finished, daddy lay back and sighed a deep sigh and died.

The atmosphere in the room was so peaceful. Somehow I didn't react either way, I don't know if it was just shock that he had died or that there was something which occurred that made everyone so calm, or possibly both.

I can honestly say, I was so blessed to be there to experience what happened and such helped me to appreciate the great gift of kindness my mother carried out to assist my daddy to leave us all in such a quiet and beautiful way'.

This story exemplifies the selflessness of Kitty's mum who while in a place of brokenness she permitted her husband to die in great peace. *'The image of daddy's serene acknowledgement of all of us who prayed by his bedside and the Virgin image has had a profound effect upon all of us who had gathered in the room the night daddy died'*, Kitty added in an affirming tone.

Unlike the experience of Kitty and her family, sometimes it may be difficult to carry out an act of kindness, depending on where a person is at. To care is one thing but to act is another; therefore, such must consider the person, the situation and the openness of the other one wishes to help or support. When tragedy occurs, whether it is an accident, an illness or a fatality, what is the instant reaction of most people?

Generally, the immediate reaction is to embrace the person's affected with the pain, sickness and/or loss and then to move into an active role where people begin to do whatever is needed to help. Sometimes such assistance can be as simple as just being present; making sandwiches and serving tea to those who visit as a mark of respect; bring flowers and cards and pray with and for those in need.

So while there are acts which can be applied as verbal, written, active and so on, frequently, it is never to be witnessed the feelings so many people have one another. When people are lonely, sad, and sick and/or more, a card with a good wish can have a huge impact upon the person suffering. A big bear hug can work wonders; just that feeling that someone cares is so powerful.

Kindness can never be measured; no cost can ever be assigned to such a wonderful deed. The act of kindness does not stop as a means of support for people but can be of great support and comfort to animals in need. And furthermore, believing in the green issue and recycling, reflect the profound love for the planet by those who embrace the acts of kindness and consideration for life and living. Sometimes, we are intrigued when we become aware of the rainbow showing off its rays of colours reflective of the healing power of the Angels. And as a feather falls it may transpire that a message of affirmation has come one's way. As mentioned previously sounds and lyrics can convey some contradictions worthy of note, in that such can alert us to think and to notice things that confront us frequently.

Feathers, Sounds and Colours

Have you ever met someone whom you would like to help but for some reason their guard built around them prevents anyone from reaching them. After Anna's young son was killed in a traffic accident, she withdrew from all those around her. She couldn't perceive that life could ever move from the place she had found herself after Jamie was buried.

Resentment played a big part in her everyday life. The barrier around her was so powerful that family, friends, neighbours and clergy were fearful of what the outcome would be for Anna. One evening, when sitting by the grave in the dim lit cemetery, Anna's husband Mark watched as she sobbed. As she did so, she heaved awkwardly, as if her heart was about to burst open. All of a sudden, she sat upright and turned towards Mark indicating that she needed him to join her. *'I was shocked! We had been visiting there every night since the Jamie was buried and she always just sat there in the same spot at the same time every evening, just staring into the clay'*, Mark said.

After a long pause he continued:

'Out of the blue, Anna reached out for my hand. It was the greatest gift I had received. As I moved close to her, she pointed to a feather which had landed on a wee truck near the headstone. I shrugged my shoulders. 'It's just a feather', I thought but didn't say anything'. With tears now running down this macho man's face it was easy to perceive the mix of pain and joy he experienced. On the one hand, Anna had moved to a place where Mark felt wanted. There was a sense of belonging and on the other hand, he couldn't understand why she was so excited about a feather. As I was about to talk, Mark interrupted, *'You know what, that one wee feather had such an impact on my Anna. I don't think I even needed to understand the meaning or the significance of the tiny little white feather sitting on the truck . . . then she began to explain to me that the feather represented the presence of an Angel. Since that day, the transformation in Anna has been great. She is getting stronger and stronger and she even has started to realise that I am hurting, too!'*

I was left speechless.

The presence of something as tiny as a feather, had a wonderful impact upon Anna and Mark, and has helped them to share, to listen and to embrace each other. Recently, Anna and Mark were purported to say that their loss will always be with them and knowing that the Angels are with them is so wonderful. They also believe that their wee son is an Angel who will constantly travel the journey of life with them as he will flit from shoulder to shoulder twenty four seven, three six five! Imagine being so sure that your very own is an Angel who accompanies you day and daily.

In the silence many people experience something extraordinary or what some people refer to as a coincidence may occur; when either the words of a song confirm a thought in the mind, or a letter or card arrives by post with words which affirm and embody the belief that Angels are near.

Lynn told how words in a dream meant so much to her. *Just over two years ago, my mother died. For a long time I kept myself so busy I didn't have time to feel sorry for myself. Then one night, Monday week past actually (I am so sure because I recorded my dream), in the dream my mother was in the car with me. As we drove homeward there was the most awesome rainbow stretching and creating what seemed like a tunnel which I had to drive through. The rays of light emanating around the car were similar to those depicting the healing energy of the Lord of Divine Mercy. As I drove through the tunnel of light there ahead in the sky were the words, 'Jesus, in Thee, I trust.'*

My mother began the Chaplet and I responded energetically. The happening was a replica of how we used to carry out this practice when we travelled together. The rays of colour began to leave the rainbow. First, a flame of blue light came towards us, followed by a sweet green light being pushed along by a flashing white light which penetrated both of us. The overwhelming heat of the rays of light was so powerful that I pulled in along the side of the road and turned to hug my mother. Suddenly, a passing vehicle blew a loud sounding horn which awakened me, bringing me swiftly back to reality. The dream was so poignant that I realised that I had been trying to deny the need to grieve and let go.'

Such stories are examples of how feathers, sounds and colours may actually be tools alerting us to the realisation that life is full of signs and symbols which affirm and empower us more often than we may believe.

With reference to colours, very often when we are alerted to a particular colour it may signify the presence of God's healing power. Rays of coloured light empower and enlighten our spirit. The spectrum of colours within a rainbow corresponds to the rays associated with the healing energies of the Angels e.g.

Crystal reflects transformation and intuition

Red denotes empowerment and strength.

Orange indicates acceptance to change.

Yellow signifies renewed inner health and power.

Green symbolises physical healing and evolution.

Blue represents protection and harmony.

Violet is indicative of ultimate balance of body, soul and mind.

When one or a number of intermittent rays of light are apparent such is an affirmation of the healing energy of the Angels. Persons deeply connected with the Angels may frequently be aware of such experiences. Yet, this does not imply that such experiences are for the select few. So don't become despondent if such seems alien when beginning to opening oneself to the Angels.

When we become sensitive to symbols, signs, sounds and colours it is then we are invited to embrace all that is good. Something as simple as a feather may indeed have a powerful positive influence on a person in need.

The power of sound whether silent or vocal can provide a profound sense of affirmation. Colours of various hues may have a great effect when one is seeking some kind of a sign.

Very often we encounter moments clothed in tears and fears and such simple, yet, extraordinary experiences bolster our fragile and vulnerable self.

# Tears and Fears

Tears frequently fall, as a consequence of sadness and/ or joy. Occasionally, when we receive good news we automatically react to an overwhelming sense of happiness. Ironically, when we call upon the Angels they too cry with joy.

When tears fall, we silently utter liquid prayers. We offer prayers relating to happiness, sadness, illness, tragedy, pain, fun, celebration, surprise and atonement.

As raindrops fall upon the earth, frequently such is a reminder of the tears the Angels might shed when rejected by those whom they desire to serve. Yet, when rain drops glisten it is then we are reminded of the loving energy the Angels wish to share with God's creation.

Clouds embody the love and hope of the higher power of the Creator who wants nothing only the best for us, His creation. Clouds teasing the over blanket of the sky as fluffy balls of cotton wool drift by, playing hide and seek with the sun.

Sunshine reflects the light of life resonating from the heavens, God's affirmation to us. Despite the sun occasionally being clouded over, just like God the sun is ever present. So too, the moon is determined to make its presence felt as the night light glows to guide and protect the world and all that inhabits such. Twinkling stars reflect the beauty present in heaven; night stars are the good-night kisses from God and the Angels.

God is forever present in the sun and the moon, the stars and the clouds, in the rain and the snow, in the warmth and the cold. Sometimes, the snow and the cold can remind us of the fears and the worries which confront us and affect us negatively. As the snow brings with it a depth of cold air, so too, when we encounter fear we become scared and insecure.

But we are repeatedly encouraged to remember that anything that may disturb your peace cannot be of God. The love and affection God has for us is unconditional and ever merciful.

Some examples of that which can unsettle us may come in the form of chain letters, e-mails, texts and others. Whatever form, whatever appearance, whatever the contents: never be afraid to make the appropriate choice . . .

On no account, be led by others; be big enough to make your own decision. No harm can come as a consequence of stopping or breaking a chain letter. Anything that is good is of God and that which is unsettling or disturbing will never carry any ultimatum, e.g. *'Copy this nine times and pass on to others: light a blessed candle, post a number of requests on an altar and pass on in a specific time to others';*

'*Read this and pass on and your request will be granted*' and so on.

It's amazing how disconcerting chain letters can be . . . it's strange how people may feel that they must adhere to such directives. Therefore, those who post chain letters may quite innocently believe they have a role to play, or are afraid of the possible consequences of not fulfilling the request sent to them. However, for the unafraid individual who has the ability to make a decision and overlook the need to do as requested, this will not pose a difficult choice.

But there will always be the vulnerable people who may be hesitant to stop the chain as Anne tells us: '*I was asked to receive five Angels into my home. In the letter the directive included that an altar was to be set up, a service was to be held with a blessed candle to be lit and the names of three people whom I would pass this request onto within a number of days, was to be placed on the altar.*

Alarm bells were ringing.

Yet, I was terrified.

I didn't know . . . I did know what to do but I kept telling myself I didn't know what to do. I went out to seek help and was advised not to entertain this practice and not to worry, just take the Holy Water and bless the house, a woman told me.

But I was still scared that something would happen to me or my family. I did bless the house, and, I mean, really blessed the whole place: upstairs, downstairs, room by room and asking my Angel to help me and the only reason I stopped was because the phone rang.

A friend rang to see if I was okay.

I told her I was blessing the whole place and she gently calmed me down saying, 'Here, you don't have to go through every nook and cranny with the Holy Water, God knows by your act and your intention what you are requesting. Just call upon your Angel and you will be fine', she continued. This was great; it was as if my Angel was reassuring me that all is well.

Since that day I have never had any worries when confronted by chain letters. I just dispose of them by giving them back to where they came from or burning them. I now believe that anything that creates worry, discord or any disharmonious thought is not of God . . . . I can't believe that I fell for that. But you know what: the innocent request was apparently based in spirituality. The request was really well presented, but with an underlying false promise it could be gained through following such directives.

It is seven years since this occurred and since that day everything has been good. In actual fact, after breaking the chain many graces and blessings have been received not just by me but members of my family too'.

Ultimately, life and living continually challenges each and everyone to consider, *'Whose life is it, anyway?'* In being alert to ourselves we can permit ourselves to recognise when Angels whisper to remind us that it is a personal responsibility to live life to the full, within a balance of body, soul and mind.

A

Few

Messages

From

The

Angels

As Angels, we wish to serve.

As Angels, we must not be worshipped or adored.

As Angels, we are God's messengers!

As Angels, we wait for you to call.

As God's heavenly aides we wait, we listen.

As Angels, we invite you to TRUST

As Angels, we remind you good is of God.

As Angels, we bring inner peace, just call.

As Angels, we remind you God's love is unconditional; it is for you, for me, for all!

Archangel Michael brings a ray of blue light to guard and protect.

Archangel Raphael brings a ray of emerald green light to heal and empower.

Archangel Gabriel brings a ray of white light to purify thought and communication.

Call upon your Angel

Call upon your Angel, chosen to care for you,
A messenger given you by God,
To guide you day and night!
The Angelic spirit by your side,
Knows your inner hurts and pain,
A guardian whom you never see
Yet, is constantly by your side!

Call upon your Angel, whose presence is serene,
An Angel filled with the love of God
Who will guard you from all harm.
A guardian whom you never see
Waiting patiently for your call!

Call upon your Angel, the spiritual one of God,
Sent on the day that you are born;
To walk the journey of life with you,
One who will lift you when you fall!
An Angel ready to respond to you
When you allow yourself to call!

Call upon your Angel, waiting in the wings,
Sent from heaven to guard you,
And to protect you from all harm.
So, call upon your Angel when you feel the need,
Thank your God who sent you
This spirit friend of Love!

As my youngest grand-daughter, Caoimhe told me, after a sleep over: *'Granny, last night when I was in Roisin's bed, the Angels were flying around the roof, there were twinkling lights and the Angels were singing out loud,* 'bualadh bos' which is Irish, the translation for which is *'Clap your hands/round of applause'.*

I wish to dedicate the following prayer:

'Prayer to our Angel Guardian' to my grandchildren, Cristiona, Cormac and Caoimhe and their cousins Jordan, Garbhan and Kayla.

Prayer to our Guardian Angel

Angel of God, my guardian dear,
to whom God's love commits me here:
ever this day be at my side,
to light and guard, to rule and guide, Amen.

As the image of the *'Divine Mercy'* brings solace and peace to many who seek help and support, it seems appropriate to include the prayer of petition recited in honour of this wonderful all merciful and forgiving, heavenly Father.

Chaplet of Divine Mercy

1. Begin with the Sign of the Cross, one Our Father, one Hail Mary and The Apostles Creed.

2. Then on the Our Father Beads say the following:

    Eternal Father, I offer You the Body and Blood, Soul and Divinity of Your dearly beloved Son, Our Lord Jesus Christ, in atonement for our sins and those of the whole world.

3. On the 10 Hail Mary Beads say the following:

    For the sake of His sorrowful Passion, have mercy on us and on the whole world.

    (Repeat steps 2 and 3 for all five decades).

4. Conclude with *(three times)*: Holy God, Holy Mighty One, Holy Immortal One, have mercy on us and on the whole world.

    Use these prayers in time of need, in time of thanksgiving, in time of stress, worry or loneliness. Prayers are for every one's use, irrespective of faith tradition; everyone has 'free will, free choice' to seek help. The invitation is to permit oneself to become open in mind and heart and attain that which assists in experiencing wholeness of self!

Angels whisper—
Angels do come—Just Call!

About the Author

Kate O'Kane lives in N. Ireland and is married with three grown up children and three grandchildren. After leaving school, she entered a Convent. In her early adulthood, she managed a boutique which led to many trips to London. Through life she struggled with ill-health which caused her to give up a career in Educational Administration and Finance. However, *'when one door closes, another opens'*, and she found writing poetry and prose a therapeutic, challenging and enjoyable outlet. During a period of ill-health she studied Counselling; after which she returned to university as a mature student, where she gained a degree in Psychology. This led to further studies in Theology and Spirituality. Through periods of illness she explored the effects of alternative and complementary medicines and therapies. As a practising Roman Catholic she owns a profound sense of Faith. Life's experiences have permitted her to grow in awareness of the effects of the joys and sorrows of everyday life and living. With research into the concept of Angels, she has embraced the spiritual support God provides through such a medium. She continues to embrace life in whatever form or guise it may appear. This is reflected in her thoughtful and insightful writing which she wishes to share as a source of consciousness in relation to those opening to the belief that Angels can have a positive impact upon one's ultimate desire for wholeness of self. God provides for our needs—we have choice to believe and to respond!